UTAH
WOMEN

UTAH WOMEN

Pioneers, Poets & Politicians

EMILY BROOKSBY WHEELER

THE
History
PRESS

Published by The History Press
Charleston, SC
www.historypress.com

Copyright © 2019 by Emily Brooksby Wheeler
All rights reserved

First published 2019

Manufactured in the United States

ISBN 9781467142427

Library of Congress Control Number: 2019947301

To my grandmothers, mother and daughters, all remarkable Utah women

CONTENTS

Acknowledgements   9

Part I. On the Frontier   **11**
1. Chipeta: Ambassador for Peace   13
2. Emmeline B. Wells: A Voice for Women   19
3. Biddy Mason: From Slave to Philanthropist   26
4. Matilda Dudley Busby: Enterprising Pioneer   31
5. Mother Mary Augusta: Adventurous Educator   37
6. Emma Dean Powell: The Explorer's Wife   42
7. Martha Hughes Cannon: A Healthier Utah   49
8. The Bassett Sisters: Outlaw Queens   55
9. Claire H. Ferguson: The Girl Deputy   60
10. Georgia Lathouris Magerou: Mining Camp Grandmother   64

Part II. New Frontiers   **71**
11. Maud May Babcock: The First Lady of Utah Drama   73
12. Zitkála-Šá: Making Music for Her People   79
13. Kanab's All-Female City Council: No Laughing Matter   84
14. Maud Fitch: Daredevil Hero   88
15. Domitila Rivera de Martinez: A Path Home   94
16. Almeda Perry Brown: Faith and Science   99
17. Minerva Teichert: Painting Stories   106
18. Kuniko Muramatsu Terasawa: Voice of the Japanese
    in World War II   111

CONTENTS

19. Marjorie Redding Christiansen: Fly Like a WASP 116
20. Mignon Barker Richmond: Lifting Utah's Children 120

Part III. Beyond Frontiers **125**
21. Ruey Hazlet Wiesley: Growing Peace 127
22. Alene Dalton: The Story Princess 131
23. Juanita Brooks: Nothing but the Truth 135
24. Ivy Baker Priest: Making Ends Meet 140
25. Mary Lucille Perkins Bankhead: A New Genesis 145
26. Kate B. Carter and Helen Z. Papanikolas: Saving History 150
27. Chieko Nishimura Okazaki: Teaching Hope 156
28. Emma Lou Thayne: Poet of Peace 161
29. Barbara Greenlee Toomer: A World without Barriers 165

Notes 171
Bibliography 177
Index 185
About the Author 189

ACKNOWLEDGEMENTS

T hank you to the many people who helped make this book possible: the archivists and librarians at Brigham Young University L. Tom Perry Special Collections, the Church History Library of the Church of Jesus Christ of Latter-day Saints, the Denver Public Library, Dixie State University Library Special Collections, the Sisters of the Holy Cross Congregational Archives and Records, University of Utah J. Willard Marriott Library Special Collections, Utah Division of State History Research Center and Utah State University Special Collections and Archives; the members of the Cache Valley Chapter of the League of Utah Writers and UPSSEFW and especially Chadd VanZanten; Dan, Karen and Tim for their feedback on the manuscript; my family for their patience and support; and Artie Crisp and the staff at The History Press for believing in the project.

PART I

ON THE FRONTIER

The western frontier was harsh, gritty and challenging—a man's world, but a woman's world too. Women in the West enjoyed freedoms unavailable to their eastern sisters, like voting, owning land and pursuing careers in medicine or law. The frontier also had plenty of opportunities for the quieter occupations that women often pursued without fanfare, such as nursing, teaching and mothering. In large and small ways, women shaped Utah and the West alongside their fathers, brothers and husbands.

Utah was unusual among frontier states and territories because of the dominant role the Church of Jesus Christ of Latter-day Saints (Mormons) played in its history, but it still shared many features of the Old West: Native Americans struggling against the loss of their lands; mountain men and explorers forging trails westward; miners dreaming of wealth in boom-and-bust towns; and lawmen, desperados and cattle barons battling for control of towns and rangelands. Women played a role in all of these events.

Some of the women in this volume are well-known heroes, with statues and memorials, their accomplishments found in textbooks. Others are almost lost to history, saved only by a document or two that happened to survive the years. And perhaps that is what makes them so interesting: they represent many other women whose voices are silent to us but whose stories were nonetheless as remarkable as the women featured in these pages.

Chapter 1

CHIPETA

Ambassador for Peace

In 1845, a band of Utes came across an abandoned Kiowa Apache village. The inhabitants of the village had been massacred, probably by an enemy tribe, but the Utes found one survivor in the ruined camp: a two-year-old girl. They took her in and named her Chipeta. The little girl would play an important role in negotiating the future of her adopted people.

Chipeta was born just a few years before the Utes' world changed forever. The change had been on the horizon for some time. Since the early 1800s, the United States and Spain (later Mexico) had disputed ownership of the Rocky Mountains in what would become Colorado and Utah—the traditional home of the Utes.

Prior to the 1840s, fur trappers, explorers and Spanish traders made occasional intrusions into the Utes' territory, but the Utes still lived independently. They traveled in groups called bands, hunting and fishing in the mountains and meadows that had been their home for centuries.

In 1847, a group of pioneers from the Church of Jesus Christ of Latter-day Saints (Mormons) arrived in the Rocky Mountains, fleeing religious persecution in the East. They were the first of many permanent settlers. The following year, the United States won the Mexican-American War and took control of a vast swath of territory extending across the Ute lands to the West Coast. The Utes had just become part of the United States of America, though they were not recognized as citizens. In the same year, gold was discovered in California, bringing a flood of people west in 1849.

Ouray and Chipeta in 1880. *Brady-Handy photograph collection, Library of Congress, Prints and Photographs Division.*

At first, these changes had little impact on Chipeta's life. She grew up with the Uncompahgre Utes on the edge of the newly delineated Utah Territory. Established trails took most migrants north or south of her home. She came to know a young half-Ute, half-Apache man named Ouray. Ouray had been married, but his wife died, leaving him with an infant son. Chipeta helped care for the young boy, and Ouray was impressed with her. In 1859, when she was sixteen and he was twenty-six, she and Ouray married.

On the edge of their world, in what would soon be called Colorado, prospectors had discovered gold in 1858. The previously ignored Ute lands were now of great interest to the United States government.

In 1860, Ouray's father died, leaving Ouray as the leader of his band. The next year, Colorado became its own territory, carved out of the Utah and Kansas territories, and Ouray's people were a part of it. Tensions heightened between the native peoples and the settlers, fueled by the desire of each group to use the land for its own purposes. The government assigned Indian agents to the Utes to help prevent conflict. Explorer and mountain man Kit Carson was friends with Ouray and Chipeta and recommended Ouray as an interpreter and liaison for the Indian agent. Ouray had spent his childhood in New Mexico and spoke Spanish, English, Ute and Apache, and he understood both white and Native American culture.

This put Ouray and Chipeta in a difficult situation where they were viewed with mistrust by their own people and by the Indian agents. Adding more heartache to their lives, Ouray's only son from his first marriage was kidnapped by another tribe, and the Utes were never able to find him.

Chipeta did not have any children. She mourned the loss of her foster son and wanted to stay close to Ouray. Though Ute wives were usually not involved in their husbands' travels or business, Chipeta accompanied Ouray on his journeys. While he conducted formal meetings with men, Chipeta befriended the wives and other women and gathered more informal—and honest—opinions about problems with white settlers, the U.S. government and other tribes.

But no matter what Ouray and Chipeta did to keep the peace, they could not help their people keep their lands. In 1863, the Utes were forced into the first of several treaties, the Treaty of Conejos, giving up their territories on the eastern slopes of the Rocky Mountains. Because of his leadership role among the Utes, Ouray was asked to help keep the peace between his people and the white settlers streaming into the Ute homelands. This was a difficult and thankless task, especially when the government failed to keep its promise to make payments of money and cattle and to protect the remaining Ute lands from settlers and miners.

In 1869, prospectors trespassed on Ute lands and found gold in the mountains. Once again, the government stepped in to get the lands from the Utes. Ouray, Chipeta and several other native leaders met with the government officials. The Utes refused to give up any more land and insisted the trespassers be removed from their lands, as the government had promised. The government's representative, Felix R. Brunot, tried to change their minds. He finally made it clear that the Utes could either sell their land or lose it by force. Ouray later said that negotiating with the government was like a wounded bison negotiating with a hunter—the best he could do was minimize the pain and loss.

The Utes ceded the mountainous regions of Colorado with the understanding that they would still be allowed to hunt there and that the land would only be used for mining. The miners scurrying into the territory failed to keep either promise—establishing towns and blocking the Utes from hunting—and the government failed to enforce the agreement. Like Ouray's wounded bison, the Utes were bleeding out.

Ouray and Chipeta traveled to Washington, D.C., to finalize the Brunot Treaty of 1873. Chipeta was the only woman to attend the negotiations or the formal ceremonies, which included a meeting with President Ulysses S. Grant. The government named Ouray as the chief of the Utes and allotted him a house on the new reservation with a small stipend, leading other Utes to question his motives. They did not understand that resistance against the U.S. government could mean a massacre. Chipeta still managed to remain on good terms with the other bands, even when they would not talk to her husband, and she negotiated peace with those who wanted to kill him.

Chipeta protected Ouray from violence, but she could not convince all the Utes to accept peace with the white settlers, and the miners, settlers and politicians of Colorado did nothing to help the issue. Colorado governor Frederick Walker Pitkin won his 1878 election with the slogan "The Utes must go!" Nathan Meeker, the Indian agent assigned to the White River band of Utes, tried to force farming and Christianity on a people who were attempting to preserve their traditions and culture. Considering them "savage" and uncultured, he plowed under a field that was used to raise their prized racing ponies. The exact details of what happened next are a mystery, but Meeker telegraphed for military aid, saying that he had been attacked and driven from his home. Some of the White River Utes then attacked Meeker, killing the men in his party and taking the women captive. The war that Ouray and Chipeta had sacrificed so much to prevent had come.

Ouray considered taking up arms, going out to die with his people in one final stand, but Chipeta talked him out of it. Instead, she and Ouray negotiated for the release of the female captives, and Chipeta cared for the women until they were returned to their towns. Later legends said she rode single-handedly to rescue them herself, and though that is an exaggeration, she still probably saved their lives.

Despite Chipeta's efforts, Coloradans screamed for blood—even for the extermination of the entire Ute people. A delegation of Utes was summoned to Washington, D.C., to discuss the fate of their people, and Ouray and Chipeta were foremost among them. While newspapers in Colorado suggested lynching parties to eliminate the Utes, in Washington, D.C., Chipeta found herself viewed as a romantic heroine, the subject of exaggerated stories and poems. Chipeta was celebrated by dignitaries from Europe and called—sometimes mockingly—the Queen of the Utes.

The meeting in Washington, D.C., was not a friendly negotiation, though. The government had already decided that the Colorado Utes would be moved to the desolate wilderness of eastern Utah to join the Utes already living there. Ouray and Chipeta had no choice but to agree—it was that or watch their people be swept away by the flood of mob violence

These Utes from Colorado were forced to leave their homes and join the Utes living on reservations in Utah. *J.F. Jarvis, Library of Congress, Prints and Photographs Division.*

and military action awaiting them in Colorado. Amidst the fanfare of the event, Ouray put aside the white men's clothes he sometimes wore and never touched them again.

All the leaders of the Colorado Utes had to sign the 1880 Ute Agreement by the end of the year. Ouray was chosen to take the treaty to each band for their signatures, but he succumbed to illness during the effort and died. The other Utes considered ignoring the treaty until one of Ouray's opponents was struck by lightning.[1]

So, Chipeta moved with her people to Utah, following the Utes' own Trail of Tears, mourning and weeping for the home they left behind. Even in eastern Utah, they were not left in peace and lost more sections of their reservation. Living on poor, dusty land, her people sank into poverty.

Many of Chipeta's former white admirers blamed her for her dire situation, perhaps uncomfortable to see the former "Queen of the Utes" starving along with the people she had tried to save from violence. She insisted, "What is good enough for my people is good enough for me."[2] She later remarried and adopted several children. In her old age, she lost her sight, but she was still known for her kindness and hospitality to Utes or whites who came to her door. She died in 1924, the same year that all Native Americans were granted U.S. citizenship. Colorado later removed her body from Utah and brought it to be buried beside Ouray.

Chapter 2

EMMELINE B. WELLS

A Voice for Women

In February 1899, Utah sent a ten-woman delegation to the meeting of the National Council of Women of the United States in Washington, D.C. There, they would be mingling with prominent members of the women's suffrage movement, including Susan B. Anthony. Unlike many of their eastern sisters, the women of Utah had the vote, but they wanted to see women across the country have the same right. Among the Utah delegates were prominent Utah women like writer and educator Susa Young Gates; actress, teacher and nurse Zina Young Card; and Hannah Kaaepa, Hawaiian immigrant and representative of the Hawaiian Queen Liliuokalani. Among this congregation of remarkable Utah women, the one most responsible for bringing all of them there was seventy-year-old Emmeline B. Wells.

Emmeline Blanche Woodward was born on a leap year day, February 29, 1828. Even as a young child in Massachusetts, she longed to do something noteworthy with her life—to be known and remembered. Her father died when she was four years old, leaving her mother a widow with several children to care for. Despite this, Mrs. Woodward made certain that Emmeline not only got a basic education but also went to a private boarding school where she could develop her intellectual gifts.

When Emmeline visited home at age fourteen, she learned that her family had joined one of the many new religious movements that sprung up during what has been called the Second Great Awakening: a time of religious excitement in the United States. When Emmeline returned to school, her friends and associates were horrified to learn of her

Utah delegation to the Triennial National Council of Women held
in Washington, D.C., in February 1899. *Left to right, top to bottom:*
Martha Horn Tingey, Minnie J. Snow, Ann M. Cannon, Emmeline
B. Wells, Susa Young Gates, Mabel Snow, Zina Young Card, Lulu L.
Greene Richards, Lucy B. Young and Hana Kaaepa. *From* The Young
Woman's Journal *10, no. 5 (1899).*

family's new beliefs. She said, "Were they [the other students] not harassing me on every side? Did they not tear me from my beloved home and the arms of a tender parent."[3] Her diary is unclear on the details, but it seems that a teacher or perhaps even a suitor held her against her will. She recorded that "the Good Spirit interposed and provided a way for me to be released from the hands of a cruel guardian who pretended so <u>much</u> respect for me that he did not wish for me to associate with my own mother and sister."[4]

When she finished school, she returned home to her family. Upon investigating their new beliefs, she turned her back on the warnings of her former classmates and friends and joined her mother and sisters as members of the Church of Jesus Christ of Latter-day Saints, also known as Latter-day Saints or Mormons. The church's doctrine built on the idea that it was restoring the church of Jesus's days to the earth, but its claims of modern angelic visits, prophets and new scriptures called the Book of Mormon made it controversial.

Within a year, Emmeline was teaching school in Massachusetts and met fellow Latter-day Saint James Harris. With the encouragement of their families, they were married in 1843. Both were only fifteen years old. Local hostility toward Latter-day Saints continued, so in 1844, the young bride and groom traveled with his parents to the Latter-day Saint headquarters in Nauvoo, Illinois, a city perched on the Mississippi River at the edge of the frontier. In the five years since the Latter-day Saints had fled there to escape persecutions in Missouri, they had drained the malaria-ridden swamps and expanded the city to include twelve thousand people, making it as large as Chicago at that time. Church leader Joseph Smith welcomed Emmeline to Nauvoo by shaking her hand, and she said, "The one thought that filled my soul was, I have seen the prophet of God, he has taken me by the hand."[5]

But Nauvoo was not the haven Emmeline had hoped for. An anti-Mormon mob killed Joseph Smith shortly after she arrived. Emmeline's in-laws, disenchanted, left the Church of Jesus Christ of Latter-day Saints and the region. During this turmoil, Emmeline gave birth to a son, who died at six months old. Her husband, desperate for work, left his mourning wife and headed north up the Mississippi River. Emmeline longed for his return. She recorded that one evening, a steamboat arrived at the city. "O how my youthful heart fluttered with hope." She ran out to meet the passengers and thought she saw James but said, "I found I was deceived by the darkness....O God grant that he may soon return for my heart is braking [sic]."[6]

Emmeline never saw or heard from James again.

Whether her husband had died or abandoned her, Emmeline found herself desperately alone in a community in turmoil. She had believed that she would always have James there to support her and longed for her mother and sisters far away in Massachusetts. But she was not one to give up once she had chosen her course. Though only a little over five feet tall and perhaps one hundred pounds, she was a fighter. She stayed in Nauvoo and returned to teaching to support herself.

Brigham Young emerged as the new leader of the Latter-day Saints. One of the other leaders in the church was an older man named Newel K. Whitney. He predicted that Emmeline was going to do great things. He told her about the concept of plural marriage—that, as in the Old Testament, God approved of men having more than one wife to build a righteous people—and then asked Emmeline to be his third wife. Polygamy was practiced only in secret at the time, but Emmeline agreed to it. At about the same time, Brigham Young announced a new move for the Latter-day Saint people: a migration to the Rocky Mountains.

Emmeline, now part of the large, extended Whitney family that included eight wives, left Nauvoo in 1846 for Winters Quarters in Nebraska and began the journey to the Utah Territory in 1848. Emmeline found herself sleeping on the ground in tents, sometimes with rain, snow or hail falling outside, and riding in the wagon or walking over muddy trails for hundreds of miles. Life continued as they went, with the women cooking and washing and mending clothes, while the men repaired broken wagons and rescued animals lost or trapped in mud holes. When they could, the Latter-day Saints enjoyed music, dancing and worship services. Emmeline had one daughter born in the back of a wagon on the journey. A second daughter was born in Salt Lake City in 1850. When this infant was just six weeks old, Newel K. Whitney died at age fifty-five.

Once again, Emmeline became a teacher to support herself, but life in the 1800s was incredibly difficult for a single woman with young children, and Emmeline was lonely. She approached Daniel H. Wells, a good friend of her second husband and a practitioner of plural marriage, and asked to be added to his family. He agreed, and she became his seventh wife.

Emmeline and Daniel had a fairly distant relationship at first, with Emmeline living apart from him and feeling he did not need or want her. Over time, however, they became close, and their marriage produced three more daughters. Emmeline focused her attention and energy on her children and her home, though she—who enjoyed stimulating talk and good company—often felt lonely and depressed.

During this quiet time in her life, things were not quiet for the Latter-day Saint settlers in the Utah Territory. The gold rush of 1849 had brought an influx of outsiders into their refuge, and the completion of the transcontinental railroad in 1869 brought even more. The Latter-day Saints had hoped to be left alone in Utah, but that was not to be. Some visitors were just passing through, some came drawn by whatever opportunities they saw in the West and many came to gawk at the "Mormons" and speculate about the stories they had heard about their harems of wives. The feeling against polygamy grew so strong that many equated it with slavery, calling slavery and polygamy "the twin relics of barbarism."

Latter-day Saint women responded to these heated feelings with the publication of their own newspaper, called the *Woman's Exponent*. It dealt with many topics but often served as a platform for polygamous women to voice their support of the institution. Emmeline had always had a gift for poetry and writing and quickly became a popular contributor to the newspaper. In 1872, she took over as editor from the newspaper's founder, Louisa Lulu Greene. At only twenty-two years old, Louisa had been the first female editor west of the Mississippi, and when Emmeline took over, she remained the only female editor in the West. The *Exponent* was considered the most influential newspaper in the Utah Territory, and Emmeline remained its editor until it stopped publication in 1914.

The *Exponent* was not just a Utah newspaper. Issues reached readers all over the country, and at a time when few people were actually listening to what Latter-day Saint women had to say for themselves about polygamy and life in Utah. The *Exponent* changed that, especially Emmeline's writing. She pointed out that women in Utah were able to vote long before most women elsewhere had that right. She also argued that Utah women had more opportunities for college education and to pursue professional goals. Utah had female doctors and lawyers, unlike most of the eastern states. She often wrote in response to leading non-Mormon women who published their negative opinions of Utah and the Latter-day Saints in eastern newspapers, engaging in a very public, but very polite, debate that was read across the United States.

Because of her written exchanges, Emmeline gained the respect of some very influential American women, including suffragettes and women's rights leaders like Susan B. Anthony and Elizabeth Cady Stanton. Their respect for her did not erase the general prejudice against Latter-day Saints and against polygamy, but it did convince them to allow Latter-day Saint women to join the national suffrage movement. Emmeline Wells took an

Left: Leading women's rights advocate Susan B. Anthony in 1870. *Mathew B. Brady, Library of Congress, Prints and Photographs Division.*

Right: Emmeline B. Wells in 1891. *C.M. Bell, Library of Congress, Prints and Photographs Division.*

active part, traveling thousands of miles to campaign around the country for women's right to vote and to represent Utah women to the government in Washington, D.C. Despite the loss of her third husband in 1891 and the death of two of her beloved daughters, she continued her tireless work. In 1893, she was asked to speak at the Chicago World's Fair.

She also helped build bridges within Utah, as even those who were opposed to the Church of Jesus Christ of Latter-day Saints or its influence in the state respected her and invited her to attend their meetings and events. Some suggested that Emmeline should be elected Utah Territorial treasurer, but women were still not allowed to hold office, despite being allowed to vote. Emmeline was determined to change that. She campaigned for several years before convincing the territorial government to open political positions to women as well. When the federal government took away women's right to vote as part of its campaign against the influence of the Church of Jesus Christ of Latter-day Saints and polygamy in 1887, Emmeline protested. She made certain that the right was included in the state constitution in 1896 when Latter-day Saint leaders compromised with the federal government, banning polygamy and direct Latter-day Saint influence on Utah government, and Utah became a state.

In 1899, after the U.S. meeting of the National Council of Women, Emmeline stepped onto the world stage, visiting London as a representative of the United States in the International Council of Women. Her roles in Utah also gave her international influence. For some time, Emmeline had been secretary of the Relief Society, an organization of Latter-day Saint women dedicated to service. In 1910, she became the Relief Society general president. One of her Relief Society projects was the storage of extra wheat for famines or emergency situations. The year 1914 saw the start of World War I, devastating agriculture and food production around the world. Emmeline's wheat storage would prove an enormous benefit to hungry soldiers and civilians. President Woodrow Wilson visited her personally to thank her for her contributions to the war effort, both through the wheat storage and through the efforts of the Relief Society to soften the suffering endured by every nation in the war. She continued these efforts to improve the lots of men and women everywhere until illness forced her to stop in 1921.

Church leaders asked her to step down from her role as Relief Society president when she became ill. She was angry, as she had expected to die in office, but she complied. She passed away just three weeks later at age ninety-three.

Chapter 3

BIDDY MASON

From Slave to Philanthropist

Bridget "Biddy" Mason started her life as a slave, but she ended it as one of California's wealthiest citizens. Her story demonstrates Utah's role as the "crossroads of the West" in the expansion of the United States.

Biddy was born in 1818, probably in Georgia, though little is known about her early life. This is the tragic situation of many enslaved African Americans, for whom accurate records were not always kept. We do know that by 1836, when Biddy was about eighteen, she was living in Mississippi on the plantation of Robert Marion Smith and Rebecca Crosby Smith. Biddy had developed a reputation as a skilled midwife, but she was still required to do backbreaking work on the plantation in addition to caring for her young daughter. During this time, she had two more daughters. The identity of their father is unknown, but rumors suggested it was Robert Marion Smith.

In 1844, Robert and his family joined the Church of Jesus Christ of Latter-day Saints. The church's founder, Joseph Smith, disliked slavery and welcomed black members into the church, but his death at the hands of a mob in 1844 left black Latter-day Saints in an uncertain position. At that time, enslaved people needed the permission of their owners to be baptized. Biddy remained illiterate throughout her life, so we do not know what her thoughts were on the Latter-day Saints or if she ever had an interest in being baptized.

Church leaders encouraged Robert to free his slaves, but he refused to do so. Instead, when he moved to the Utah Territory in 1848 as part of

Bridget "Biddy" Mason, unknown date. *Courtesy of the National Park Service.*

the Mormon migration, he took Biddy, her daughters and his other slaves with him. There were thirty-four slaves in Biddy's pioneer company, belonging to Robert and other "Mississippi Saints." The slaves were expected to do most of the work on the trek, preparing food and taking care of the camp. Thirty-year-old Biddy did her part while carrying an infant and with her two older daughters in tow. Biddy also continued her work as a healer and midwife, delivering babies born along the trail to both white and black women.

Biddy and her fellow slaves were not the first African Americans to reach Utah, as free black men had been among the mountain men who hunted and trapped in the Rocky Mountains in the early 1800s. Nor were Biddy's party the first African Americans to arrive as part of the Mormon migration. Five slaves traveled to the Salt Lake Valley with Brigham Young's vanguard party in 1847. Two of them—Jacob Bankhead and Henry Brown—died along the way and were buried, like so many other westward migrants, in unmarked graves on the prairie. Green Flake, who was both a slave and a baptized member of the Church of Jesus Christ of Latter-day Saints, supposedly drove the wagon in which an ailing Brigham Young rode when he viewed the Salt Lake Valley and uttered his famous proclamation, "This is the right place. Drive on."

So, when Biddy arrived in the Utah Territory, she found herself part of a small black community, often left on the fringes of the larger Latter-day Saint and Utah experience. Utah was admitted to the United States as a slave territory in 1850, while California was admitted as free—a balancing act playing out by Congress in an attempt to slow the steady slide toward the Civil War. In addition to the slaves taken to Utah by Latter-day Saint pioneers, some non-Mormon settlers brought slaves to the territory as well. The 1850 U.S. census lists fifty African Americans in Utah, though most historians consider that number low. About half of that number were enslaved like Biddy and her children, and half were free blacks like Jane Manning James, who had been friends with Joseph Smith in Nauvoo, or Elijah Able, who still held the position in the Latter-day Saint priesthood leadership he had received during Joseph Smith's lifetime.

Whether they were free blacks or enslaved, Latter-day Saints or not, these African Americans found themselves on the fringes of Utah society. There is little written about what their lives were like, but the historical record gives us some clues. Free people of color and slaves would have had to work hard to survive, as did their white counterparts, mostly doing farm work, often struggling to grow enough to survive. Utah law codified in 1852 required owners to educate their slaves, but it is difficult to say how often that happened, and Biddy did not benefit from it, because she never learned to read or write. The law also forbade miscegenation, or interracial marriage, which was illegal in Utah until 1963.

Some slaves were freed after they reached Utah, but until they achieved their freedom, they were subject to the whims of their owners, sometimes working in place of their owners on Latter-day Saint building projects, which all church members were expected to contribute to. Green Flake's owner gave him to the church as "tithing"; church leaders later freed him.[7] Other enslaved and free black persons contributed voluntarily. A slave called Tom Bankhead (probably actually Nathan Bankhead) was one of the men who risked his life in the famous rescue of the Willie and Martin Handcart Company, a group of Latter-day Saint migrants who were stranded in a snowstorm.[8] And some white Latter-day Saints still opposed slavery, such as a bishop who protected a runaway slave from his former owners.

But life in Utah was hard for its black residents. Alex Bankhead, a former slave who arrived in the territory in 1848, said that the Utah slaves would sometimes meet and bemoan their conditions, which were not any better than those they had known in the South. They fantasized about running away to the South—or at least to somewhere warmer—but the mountains of Utah seemed like an insurmountable barrier to escape.[9] It is easy to imagine Biddy huddled around a little stove with the other African Americans in Salt Lake City while thick drifts of snow fell outside, dreaming about lands far beyond the stormy mountain peaks. Freedom must have seemed just as far away as warmth and sunshine.

Brigham Young envisioned a Utah extending far beyond the current state's boundaries. Concerned about self-sufficiency so far from manufacturing and agricultural centers, he wanted Utah to be able to grow its own cotton and other warm-weather crops. That would mean sending Mormon colonies south, and the ideal settlers were those from among the Mississippi Saints who had grown cotton in the past. Robert Smith was one of those called to make the journey past the borders of Utah and into San Bernardino, California.

California was a free state. Any enslaved people entering California would be free from slavery forever, though most slaves did not know that. Brigham Young told Robert Smith and the other white Southerners that they should free their slaves before heading to California or let them remain in Utah. Robert refused to listen. Willing or not, Biddy and her children traveled to California with Robert in 1851.

Robert's slaves were not the only African Americans on the journey. Biddy made friends with another black woman, Liz Flake, as the party journeyed south. Some of the African Americans in the group had been freed in Utah, but with few other prospects (and perhaps a strong dislike of Utah's cold climate), they chose to try their luck with the Latter-day Saints in California. Biddy and her children served for five years in the California household of Robert Smith, apparently unaware that they were now free, or perhaps uncertain of what freedom meant or what to do with it. Robert, however, grew dissatisfied with the Church of Jesus Christ of Latter-day Saints, in part, it seems, because he was frequently chastised for not freeing his slaves. Also, his business was doing poorly. He decided he was done with California and the Latter-day Saints.

In 1855, he loaded his wagons and snuck away in the night, fleeing for the slave state of Texas with his slaves. Liz Flake and Robert Owens, a free black man from California, raised the alarm that Robert was taking his—technically freed—slaves back into slavery: essentially kidnapping them. A posse caught up to Robert before he made it out of California. He went to court to argue that his slaves wanted to stay with him and that they were, in fact, part of his family. This may have been literally true, given rumors that he was the father of some of his slaves' children. Black women could not testify in court, but the judge met with Biddy and the other enslaved women in private and, as a result of their stories, declared them all legally free in 1856, sending Robert Smith away empty-handed. It was a stroke of luck that it happened when it did. Just a year later, the Supreme Court's decision in the Dred Scott case would have kept Biddy and the others enslaved even if they lived in a free state or territory. But, at thirty-seven years old, Biddy was finally a free woman.

Biddy wasted no time making good use of her freedom. She continued her work as a nurse and midwife, earning a salary for her work for the first time in her life and delivering hundreds of babies of all ethnicities. She saved her money and used it to purchase real estate in the little town of Los Angeles. Her hard work and real estate investments were the foundation of her family's fortune. She built several small houses that she rented out, and

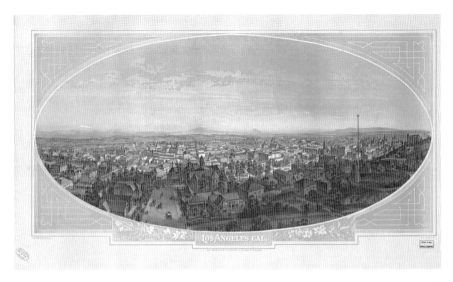

Los Angeles in 1888 when Biddy Mason took part in its growth. *Library of Congress, Prints and Photographs Division.*

as Los Angeles boomed, she sold parts of her property to invest in more lands and buildings. She became the wealthiest black woman in California and part of the state's landowning elite.

But Biddy did not forget her humble origins. She was beloved for her kindness to the poor, often visiting and nursing those in prison and feeding lines of people who would come to her home at 331 South Spring Street. She founded a school for black children, though she remained illiterate. She also helped to found the First African Methodist Episcopal Church, which is still a thriving religious community today. She died in 1891 at seventy-three years old.

It may seem that Biddy's stay in Utah was only a bad dream that she woke from when she reached California and that her time among the Latter-day Saints was one she wanted to forget. She did not show an inclination to return to Utah or be baptized as a Latter-day Saint, but when she gained her freedom and was able to choose a last name for herself, she picked Mason in honor of Amasa Mason Lyman, a Latter-day Saint leader who had overseen the settlement in San Bernardino and served as the first mayor of the city.

Ties remained strong between Southern California and Utah, though Brigham Young's dream of a Mormon enclave in San Bernardino faltered under political realities and the rush of immigration to California. Still, the impact of the early black Utah pioneers like Biddy Mason was felt in both states for generations to come.

Chapter 4

MATILDA DUDLEY BUSBY

Enterprising Pioneer

Matilda Dudley Busby knew what it meant to face hardship, but as with many of Utah's pioneer women, she met it head on and overcame it with energy and determination. Yet if it were not for a few family stories and some legal and church records, the details of her accomplishments would be lost to history, like those of many other men and women living in the nineteenth century.

Matilda was born in 1818 to Lawson and Judith Dudley, but exactly where she was born is a mystery because of the scarcity of birth records from the early 1800s. Later family accounts disagree as to whether she was from Pennsylvania or Michigan, as do censuses. The 1860 census states that she was born in Pennsylvania, while the 1880 census says Michigan. Censuses in the 1800s were completed by whomever opened the door to the census taker, so the data are only as reliable as the memory of the person at home that day and the hearing of the census taker.

The most significant event in Matilda's young life might offer the best clue about her origins. By the time of Matilda's birth, there were very few Native Americans left in Pennsylvania. In Michigan, however, the Chippewas, Ottawas and Potowatomies controlled most of the richly wooded land. And in 1819, they were pressured into ceding a large portion of that land to white settlers, angering many tribe members. This might explain what happened to the Dudleys when Matilda was only one year old.

Matilda's son would later tell family members that in 1819, Matilda's father was scalped and killed on his farm by Native Americans, who then took Matilda and Judith captive. The family story says that an older Native American man whom Judith had once been kind to took pity on the mother and child and offered to help them escape. He snuck them away from camp and brought them food.

"I'll try to come back and lead you to safety," he told Judith, "but the others suspect it's my fault you escaped, and they're angry with me, so if I don't return, you'll know that they have killed me."

Several days passed, and the man never came back. Cold, out of food and desperate, Judith snuck away, hoping she would not stumble across any of the Native Americans hunting for her. She encountered a white family moving to Ohio and traveled with them to settle there.[10]

Matilda spent most of her childhood in Ohio, which had only been a state for seven years and still was very much part of the frontier. Employment opportunities for single women were limited at this time, and no records describe how Matilda and her mother survived. Judith might have remarried, since she was still a young woman. Or perhaps she worked as a nurse. Matilda demonstrated skill as a nurse later in life, which she may have learned from her mother during their years in the frontier towns of Ohio. She seems to have had some education during this time as well, though how much was formal and how much took place at home we can only guess.

Legal records help to pin down Matilda's time and place in 1837, when, at the age of nineteen, she married Stephen Ferguson in Lucas, Ohio.

By 1840, Matilda and Stephen were living in the booming town of Cleveland, where Matilda gave birth to a son named Henry. Then, Stephen disappears from the historical record and from Matilda and Henry's lives. He may have deserted Matilda, but it is just as likely that he died, given the short life span of many frontier settlers. Ohio experienced several cholera epidemics in the 1830s and 1840s, and Stephen could have been one of the thousands who perished of this severe intestinal infection. Regardless of what happened to him, his absence left Matilda to raise their son alone.

Later in the 1840s, Matilda went by the surname Paschall, raising another mystery about her life. Unless she had another reason for living under a different last name, she must have married again, but her second husband never shows up in any records. Did Mr. Paschall die or desert her? Or did he and Matilda separate due to a disagreement? In 1849, thirty-year-old Matilda joined the Church of Jesus Christ of Latter-day Saints, and it is possible that this choice separated her from her second husband. Whatever her family circumstances, the decision to join the new religion must have been difficult, since at this time, anti-Mormon mobs had driven the Latter-day Saints from the eastern states.

A street in Salt Lake City in 1851 around the time when Matilda Dudley arrived. *Library of Congress, Prints and Photographs Division.*

Migrating west was expensive, involving buying a wagon and provisions for the long overland trip, and it took three years for Matilda to save the money to move herself and eleven-year-old Henry to Utah. It is unclear which Mormon pioneer party she traveled with or if she arranged her own way to Utah, but in 1851, she settled in the old Thirteenth Ward of Salt Lake City, located just southeast of Temple Square.

By the time of her arrival, Mormon settlers had been in the area for a few years. The settlers' farms were beginning to prosper, but many native Utes were suffering from diseases brought by the new settlers, in addition to hunger and stress from the disruption of their traditional society. Despite her family's history with Native Americans—or perhaps because of it—Matilda was concerned about the Utes' plight. She and a group of other Utah women banded together to help them by sewing blankets, clothing and other items to relieve their distress. These women had little themselves, but in their hardships, they felt empathy for others who suffered as well.

Matilda, though a single mother presumably working to support herself and her son, served as both president and treasurer of the organization, which they called the Indian Relief Society. She became known for her skill at making rugs and carpets.[11]

Brigham Young approved of the women's efforts and reorganized them into church Relief Societies in 1854. The official Latter-day Saint Relief Society had existed in Nauvoo, Illinois, but fell apart after the murder of church founder Joseph Smith. Now, Brigham Young called Matilda as Relief Society president over the women in the Thirteenth Ward, responsible not just for helping with the relief of the Native Americans but also any poor among the settlers. Matilda wrote a code of conduct for the women, one of the few opportunities we have of hearing her voice: "That we speak no evil of each other nor of the authorities of the Church but endeavor by means in our power to cultivate a spirit of union, humanity and love and that this shall be the covenant into which all shall enter who become members of this society."[12]

This, along with pioneer poet Eliza R. Snow's careful preservation of the Nauvoo Relief Society's records and spirit of sisterhood, was an early step toward the reestablishment of the church-wide Relief Society, an organization that gave women in Utah opportunities to organize and lead, as well as providing aid for those who were suffering.

Under Matilda's leadership, the women of the Thirteenth Ward Relief Society went door to door asking for donations of clothing, money or anything that could be used to help the Utes. She also organized a party in the Salt Lake City Social Hall as a fundraiser.

These efforts continued until 1857. In that year, federal troops descended on Utah to deal with the "Mormon Problem," and the frightened Mormon settlers closed ranks and retreated into forts and large settlements for protection. Though Latter-day Saint and U.S. Army leaders diffused the Utah War without any official conflict (the Mountain Meadows Massacre of California-bound Arkansas migrants occurred during this time), it brought an increased federal presence to Utah and hampered Latter-day Saint dreams of an independent state.

During the turmoil of the Utah War, Matilda Busby married her third and final husband, Joseph Busby. Matilda was Joseph Busby's second wife, making her, at age thirty-nine, a polygamist. She and Joseph had only one child, a son named George. The 1860 census shows Matilda, Henry and George living in the same household as Joseph and his other wives, everyone working together on his farm.

Joseph Busby was known to be generous to his neighbors but also stubborn and independent. He was excommunicated from the Church of Jesus Christ of Latter-day Saints for a dispute with his local church leadership about how he wanted the tithing he donated to the church to be used, though he later rejoined the church.

We know less about Matilda's activities during these decades or about her relationship with Joseph and the rest of his family. She's missing entirely

Eliza R. Snow, Utah poet and LDS Relief Society leader. *From* Biography and Family Record of Lorenzo Snow, *Salt Lake City, Utah, 1884.*

from the 1870 census, unless she was living under an assumed name because of her status as a polygamous wife. Many plural wives went on the "Mormon Underground" to avoid persecution by federal officials by using false names and moving from house to house, but this was more common in the 1880s.

The 1880 census suggests that sixty-one-year-old Matilda was living apart from her last husband, alone with her son George, Henry having married and moved away. She listed herself as a widow. Perhaps she was only counting her first husband or protecting Joseph from charges of polygamy, or maybe she was suggesting that Joseph was dead to her. Many polygamous marriages were not happy or successful, and hers could have been one of them.

Matilda supported herself and her son by working as a nurse, but she did not let her age or previous heartaches stop her ambitions. She had spent much of her life fending for herself, and it seems she was finally ready to enjoy the fruits of her hard work. Using the money she had earned, she bought and sold pieces of land around Salt Lake City in the 1880s and 1890s, slowly building her wealth through real estate investments.

At seventy years old, Matilda got involved in an even more lucrative business: mining. Of course, she did not pick up a shovel and head into the mines. Instead, she helped to open and manage one in Emery County in eastern Utah. The Beehive Reservoir Coal and Mining Company was primarily seeking coal in 1890, important for fuel in Utah and elsewhere. H.W. Hooten was the president and one of the largest shareholders in the mine, but Matilda and her sons Henry Ferguson and George Busby were also major shareholders, and together the mother and sons controlled more shares of the mine than the company president. Matilda was also the treasurer of the organization, no small responsibility.

Matilda did not just content herself with managing the money of the mining company, either. She also took an active role in helping it run efficiently. One of the ways she did this was to work with Hooten and their partner C.C. Reynolds to invent a better brake for controlling wagons going down steep hills.[13] If brakes failed on mountain roads, it did not just risk losing coal or equipment; the accident could kill the mine's employees. Matilda and the two men patented their design for a safer brake that would slow or stop the wagon automatically if it rolled down a steep grade. This made Matilda Busby one of the few known female inventors in nineteenth-century Utah.

The private life of this seventy-plus-year-old woman was not quiet either. In 1894, she traded some shares in the mine for a piece of land. The man she traded with decided the shares were not worth as much as the land and called her to a meeting with his lawyers. There, he pressured her into signing the land back over to him, threatening to have her arrested and refusing to let her leave until she did. She later took him to court, claiming he had only been able to force her to sign because she was seventy-eight years old and very feeble.[14] Her body may not have been strong, but her mind and her will certainly were. Unfortunately, the newspapers do not record how the lawsuit ended.

Matilda died in 1895, leaving behind a large estate to her sons Henry and George. Her obituary was short and sheds little light on her colorful life. Her tombstone in the Salt Lake City Cemetery reads, "She lived for others as well as herself." Besides her efforts in the Indian Relief Society, we know little about what service she might have rendered for others. Legal and government records rarely track kindness or compassion. Like most of the details of Matilda's life, history remains silent on the subject.

Chapter 5

MOTHER MARY AUGUSTA

Adventurous Educator

Members of the Church of Jesus Christ of Latter-day Saints made up the largest group of settlers in Utah during its frontier days, but they were not the only immigrants to the territory. After the discovery of gold at Sutter's Mill in California in 1848, a flood of migrants passed through Utah on their way to the gold fields. Some of these Forty-Niners decided to stay in Utah. Many of them saw opportunities in Salt Lake City in opening their own businesses to serve other westward-bound migrants. When the transcontinental railroad connecting the East and West was completed in Utah in 1869, it opened up the Utah Territory to many adventurous men and women seeking opportunities in the West.

Mining was a favorite venture of many of the men who came to the Utah Territory. Brigham Young discouraged mining for precious metals among the Latter-day Saints, as he wanted to avoid the boom-and-bust cycle and rough living it brought. He encouraged his followers to pursue a more stable foundation in agriculture instead. But Colonel Patrick Connor of the U.S. Army, who had been stationed in Utah to keep an eye on the Latter-day Saints and Native Americans, encouraged his men to mine, hoping an influx of miners would displace the two troublesome groups in his charge. Mining did not explode in Utah as it did in other places, but the land did prove rich in some valuables like silver, copper and coal. Some Latter-day Saints who had emigrated from mining regions like Cornwall and Wales used their expertise in the Utah coal mines, but many of the miners were non-Mormons, and they had their share of boom-and-bust towns in the mountains with drinking, fighting and drifting.

In the mid-1870s, this world of hard living was interrupted by an unexpected arrival. Two Catholic nuns in black habits walked from camp to camp, meeting with the miners. Perhaps more unexpectedly, the men were very interested in what these two middle-aged religious women had to say. The nuns represented another common class of migrants to Utah: those who saw the Utah Territory as a foreign missionary field. Mother Mary Augusta's efforts would help transform education and healthcare in the Utah Territory.

Mother Augusta was born in Virginia in 1830 as Amanda Anderson. When she was young, her father decided to move the family to what was then the frontier in Kansas. According to later stories, Amanda's brother was kidnapped on the journey, and their father had to pay a ransom to have him returned. Worried for his daughter's safety, Amanda's father left her to be raised by an aunt in Ohio. The aunt was a devout Catholic who, in the absence of a regular Catholic church on the frontier, had set up a chapel in her home for traveling priests. Amanda quickly developed a taste for religious life, often helping her aunt tend the sick and poor and engaging in missionary efforts with the local Native Americans. She also valued her education, riding long distances to the small frontier school.

When Amanda reached adulthood, she traveled to Notre Dame, Indiana. Notre Dame was home to the University of Notre Dame and St. Mary's College, male and female Catholic colleges, as well as the Sisters of the Holy Cross, a Catholic organization with a specific focus on education and nursing. In 1854, Amanda joined the Sisters of the Holy Cross, adopting the name Sister Mary of St. Augusta.

As Sister Augusta, her work with the poor and sick expanded, and she helped open schools in the area and taught. She also tended the sick in Indiana during an outbreak of typhoid fever, a very contagious illness that can cause pain, delirium, difficulty breathing and sometimes organ damage and death.

In 1861, with the beginning of the Civil War, the U.S. government called on the Sisters of the Holy Cross to help provide medical care to wounded soldiers in Union hospitals and aboard the hospital ship *Red Rover*. Sister Augusta had no formal medical training but plenty of hands-on practice, and she put it to good use caring for wounded soldiers from both sides of the war for four years. She also reached out to children who had been orphaned by the war. General Ulysses S. Grant came to trust Sister Augusta to treat his men in the most gruesome and dangerous conditions imaginable. Several of the other nurses from the Sisters of the Holy Cross died in their efforts to save soldiers on the battlefield.

Following the Civil War, Sister Augusta continued her work of nursing and education. She gained the attention of Father Lawrence Scanlan, the missionary priest assigned to the Catholics of Utah, in 1875. He requested her help in the distant Utah Territory. Mary Augusta, by then Mother Augusta, answered the call, traveling along with Sister Raymond by train to Salt Lake City.

The Catholic population in Utah was very small, as were the other non–Latter-day Saint denominations. The Church of Jesus-Christ of Latter-day Saints had established schools throughout its colonies in Utah, but they were religious schools, and some of the ones that provided elementary education were not very good. Father Scanlon and Mother Augusta agreed to the obvious solution: they needed a school of their own.

In the days before government-funded education, local families often had to work together to provide a school for their children. While this was not a problem for tightly knit Latter-day Saint communities, the non–Latter-day Saint population was relatively small and widely scattered. It would take a significant amount of legwork to collect the funds necessary to build a school.

Mother Augusta was undeterred. She and Sister Raymond traveled through vast stretches of unsettled territory to visit the mining camps in Utah, asking the men if they would not like a good school to send their children to. Few of the miners were married, but many hoped to be someday, and they did not like the idea of sending their children to Latter-day Saint schools. They might have even been glad to get back at a dominant culture that often looked down on them. The miners donated to the cause, and soon, Mother Augusta had her Catholic school. St. Mary's Academy opened in 1875 with one hundred students—mostly Protestants.

Brigham Young had wished Mother Augusta well in her endeavor but warned the Latter-day Saints not to send their children to her Catholic school. The school's reputation became so good, however, that some Latter-day Saint parents ignored his warnings, and the Latter-day Saint–sponsored schools scrambled to improve their offerings in response, raising the standard of education for all Utah students. One of the most famous products of Mother Augusta's Utah schools was Bernard Devoto, a prominent educator, Western historian and conservation leader. The school she founded served several generations of students until quality public education reduced the demand for private religious schools.

Mother Mary Augusta. *Courtesy of the Sisters of the Holy Cross Congregational Archives and Records.*

Mother Augusta's work in Utah did not stop with education either. The miners came to her with another problem: medical care in Utah was scarce. Mother Augusta's time in the Civil War had given her ample experience with nursing, so she set out on a new crusade. She gathered the money to rent a home and convert it into a hospital. It started with only twelve beds but soon expanded to become the Holy Cross Hospital (now the Salt Lake Regional Medical Center).

With her resources stretched thin and the demand for education and healthcare always growing, the time had come to call on more Catholic sisters to make the journey to Utah. Soon the nuns had hospitals, schools, churches and orphanages serving Utah's entire population, Latter-day Saints included.

Mother Augusta only left Utah when she was called to another important position as mother general of the Sisters of the Holy Cross in Indiana. She died there in 1907 after a life spent building Utah and other frontier communities. Her grave is marked by a U.S. Army headstone commemorating her service in the Civil War. The Sisters of the Holy Cross continue to serve Utah's needs in education, health and human welfare through the Holy Cross Ministries.

Chapter 6

EMMA DEAN POWELL

The Explorer's Wife

Nineteenth-century women were often involved in their husbands' businesses as silent, but essential, partners, and this went for the wives of explorers and adventurers as well. John Wesley Powell is a famous name in western history, but very few accounts of his adventures mention the vital role that his quiet wife, Emma Dean Powell, played in his successes.

In 1853, eighteen-year-old Emma Dean, living in Detroit, received an unusual visitor. Her half-cousin John Wesley "Wes" Powell had paddled up the Mississippi River from Illinois in a canoe and then walked through the woodlands of Michigan to visit her family. Though Michigan was still part of the frontier, Detroit was an important shipping center and already had a population of over twenty-six thousand people, many of them migrants from New England and foreign countries. Emma's father, Joseph, was a hatmaker and clerk in a hat shop. Wes's visit must have offered a refreshing break from the drudgery of life in a squalid nineteenth-century city.

Wes was twenty-one and had already begun an adventurous life. His father was a farmer and preacher, and since about the age of twelve, Wes had been left to run the farm while his father traveled to preach. The family had farmed in Ohio for a while, but their abolitionist sentiments made them unpopular with their neighbors there, and they moved farther west to Wisconsin. Wes's father expected his sons to become ministers as well, but Wes had developed a deep thirst for knowledge about the natural world, often spending his time alone devouring any book he could find, and he broke with his father to study science in Illinois. In the winters he taught

Emma Dean Powell in 1869. *National Park Service, Photographic Library, Washington, D.C.*

school and took classes from Illinois College, Wheaton College and Oberlin College, and in the summers he ventured around Missouri, Illinois, Iowa and Wisconsin, collecting interesting objects like shells, rocks and other specimens of natural history. He shared his stories and his love of science with his cousin and her family.

Quiet, petite Emma was taken with her bold cousin during his visit to Michigan, and he returned her affections. He often found excuses to travel back to Detroit and see Emma, and the two exchanged frequent letters. In them, Emma responded thoughtfully to Wes's accounts of his adventures and expressed her wish to join Wes on his travels.

As romance bloomed between Emma and Wes, the United States hurtled toward the Civil War. Wes supported abolition and regarded the war as inevitable when he heard the pro-slavery arguments of Southerners on his travels, so he enlisted with the Union in the Twentieth Illinois Volunteers, where he would serve under the command of the famous western explorer John Frémont. Perhaps spurred by the uncertainty of life during times of war, Wes took a brief leave in 1862 to come north and marry Emma. She readily agreed. They were married in her family's home, and then Emma journeyed to Tennessee with her husband to stay by his side throughout the war.

Just a few months after their marriage, Wes was injured at the Battle of Shiloh when he raised his hand to give a command to charge. A Minié ball struck his wrist and shattered the bone in his arm. In typical style of the day, the battlefield surgeons simply removed his arm at the elbow and sent him home to recover. Emma stayed by his side during the messy operation. For four months, she nursed her husband, trying to prevent infection from setting in and killing him, as was so common following battlefield injuries. Thanks to Emma's care, Wes not only recovered but also returned to the fighting, though his arm stub would cause him pain for the rest of his life. Due to his disability, he was able to get a pass for Emma to accompany him to the battlefield.

So, tiny Emma Dean Powell followed her husband into the hard life of a Civil War encampment, all the way down to Vicksburg, Mississippi. Vicksburg was a key strategic location for the Confederacy, looking out over the Mississippi River like a fortress and controlling travel on that essential waterway. The Vicksburg Campaign was a hard-fought one that lasted for two years with tens of thousands of men injured or killed. Conditions were miserable—cold and muddy in the winter and hot, humid and buzzing with mosquitoes in summer—and food and provisions were often scarce. While

Ulysses S. Grant led the Union army in a siege of the city of Vicksburg, Admiral David Farragut, who famously ordered, "Damn the torpedoes, full speed ahead!" led the navy assault on the city against ironclad ships.

Emma played her role as well, serving as a nurse in the Vicksburg hospitals. The hospitals could be in tents or in houses abandoned by local residents and were often crammed with the wounded, ill and dying. Emma treated everything from minor injuries to fatal wounds from guns and cannons. She would have seen many men who, like her husband, lost arms or legs in the battles. Work in the hospitals was dangerous, as rapidly shifting lines could bring the fighting right through where the nurses were trying to work. Yet Emma and the other nurses faithfully stayed by their posts and risked their lives to treat and comfort injured soldiers, bandaging wounds, cleaning infections, changing soiled sheets and preparing special diets in five-gallon pans.[15] General Ulysses S. Grant specifically ordered Emma to be allowed to stay at Vicksburg during the intense fighting because of her diligent work. While Emma worked with injured men, her husband fought in the trenches, studying fossils and minerals during the lulls in action.

When the war was over, Wes and Emma returned to a more settled life, with Wes teaching college in Illinois. He had turned down a more lucrative career in politics to pursue his love of science, and Emma supported him. But Wes was not one to stay still for long. His curiosity about the West drew him out to the frontier. He led expeditions of students to the Rocky Mountains to collect geology samples and explore the area.

Just as she had during the Civil War, Emma accompanied him on his travels. She was often the only woman in the party, living in rough canvas tents, cooking over campfires and helping her husband catalogue his findings. She participated in the scientific inquiries as well, keeping notes about their expedition, collecting specimens, practicing taxidermy and becoming an expert in her own right on plants of the alpine region. She did not just stay in the camp, either. Emma was one of the first women to hike Pikes Peak, joining her husband and his students in their explorations of the area. When the students returned home, she and Wes stayed in the mountains to continue their work. He resigned from his academic positions in Illinois and started the Rocky Mountain Scientific Exploring Expedition, of which Emma was a founding member and one of the commanders, which sometimes rankled the men who were expected to follow her orders. The Powells climbed the imposing Longs Peak and spent the winter of 1868 living in crude log cabins and learning from the local Utes, all while preparing for an even more ambitious journey.

Powell expedition camp in 1871. Emma would have lived in similar camps when she explored with her husband. *U.S. Department of the Interior, Geological Survey, Photo File No. PIO-H-94.*

Wes was invigorated by the success of his early expeditions and had decided to organize another historical feat: he wanted to raft down the mighty Colorado River and document the geological features and native peoples on the nine-hundred-mile trip. At that point, the entire region of the Colorado River was literally a blank spot on the map, and many people predicted Wes's proposed journey was impossible and would end in disaster. Nevertheless, Wes and Emma returned to Chicago to oversee the construction of the boats. The lead boat, to be manned by Wes, was named the *Emma Dean*. This time, Emma herself would not take part in the expedition. Instead, she waited with the rest of the country for word of the explorers, while her husband set off with a small crew down the booming river in the boat named after her.

What she heard was not good. No one knew how long the trip would take, but the first time the men checked in with a settlement near the river, they had already been beset by disaster and lost one boat. One member of the expedition quit, saying the trip was too dangerous. Wes and the rest continued on. After a long period of hearing nothing, newspapers started to speculate that Wes and his party were lost to the river. A man named John Risdon gained fame by claiming to be the only survivor of the expedition and told harrowing stories of his survival. The newspapers declared John Wesley Powell a martyr to science.

Emma knew Risdon was lying. She had helped screen and hire the members of her husband's team, and Risdon was not one of them. She could also prove that some of the facts and dates he gave were false, and she took to the newspapers to expose Risdon and express her faith in her husband's ability to survive the ordeal. Risdon's stories were too good for newspapers to pass up, until the *Chicago Tribune* printed proof that Powell was alive or had been recently: a letter sent during a short stop in Uintah Valley, Utah.

Emma had triumphed over Risdon's attention-seeking deception, but she still had to wait with the rest of the nation for proof that her husband would survive the rest of the journey. Once again, those waiting at home began to lose hope. Brigham Young—who had taken a personal interest in Powell's expedition—heard reports of wrecked boats and sent out a crew to search for any sign of the missing men. They found Wes and five of his surviving men, starving but victorious, having ridden the Colorado to St. Thomas, Utah (now part of Nevada). Three men who had deserted the expedition earlier to try to cross the desert were later found dead, believed to have been killed by local Native Americans.

Wes returned to a hero's welcome in Salt Lake City. Inspired by Wes's passion for science, Brigham Young declared that the natural sciences were important to the Rocky Mountain states and should be taught to the boys and girls of Utah.[16]

Wes's expedition made history, but he was not done. Most of his scientific research had been lost by the end of the journey. At that point, they had no longer been gathering data, just testing the limits of human ability against the fierce inhospitality of Utah's deserts. He needed to do it again. He and Emma traveled back east to raise funds for another scientific expedition down the river. In 1871, they were ready for him to make the journey again, this time with better preparations.

Emma would once again wait for Wes as he commanded the expedition, renting rooms in Salt Lake City along with Wes's sister Nellie Powell Thompson. This time, Emma was pregnant with their first and only child. The pregnancy was a difficult one, and Wes actually took a break during the expedition to visit her in Salt Lake City before hurrying back to rejoin the party. While Wes directed a more scholarly and less haphazard journey down the Colorado, Emma gave birth to their daughter, Mary Dean Powell, in Salt Lake City in September 1871. With her infant in tow, she and Nellie made the long and dangerous wagon journey south to the town of Kanab near the Utah-Arizona border in late 1871 to join her husband for his winter encampment.

On Wes's return, he was able to contribute to several national organizations, including the founding of the Bureau of American Ethnology and the United States Geographical and Geological Survey. He and Emma moved to Washington, D.C., so he could continue directing scientific surveys and societies from there.

Emma managed their household and raised their daughter in Washington, D.C., as well as being involved in her own activities. She served on the Board of Lady Managers for the 1893 Chicago World's Fair, which sponsored the Woman's Building at the exposition.[17] This was one of the first women's organizations authorized by Congress and had the goal of recognizing the achievements of women in education, the arts and applied sciences.

As Wes aged, his health declined, and the damaged nerves in his amputated stump became increasingly painful. Doctors attempted another surgery to relieve his distress, but it failed to help, and he was forced to retire, spending more time with his family in their primitive cabin in Maine. A mutual friend wrote to Emma of his deteriorating health: "Of course this condition was well known to you as far as his home life was concerned, and you, in your own way, concealed it from the curious."[18] It was perhaps these efforts to shield her husband's pride or protect him from too much strain that led some people to accuse Emma of bullying Wes in his later years.

Wes died in 1902, leaving Emma a widow with very little to survive on, as science had not been a lucrative career for their family. She applied for a widow's pension for Wes's service to his country in the Civil War. She wrote to their friend Alexander Bell, "You know better than others how faithfully he worked in the service of the government, and how much he suffered in the loss of his good right arm—on the battlefield, of his country."[19]

Her first request was denied, so she petitioned Congress directly for the pension, and it was finally granted. The pension was still a small amount to live on, even for the time: fifty dollars per month. She outlived her husband by twenty-two years, dying in 1924. She is buried beside him in Arlington National Cemetery.

Chapter 7

MARTHA HUGHES CANNON

A Healthier Utah

Martha Hughes Cannon once said, "You give me a woman who thinks about something besides cook stoves and wash tubs and baby flannels, and I'll show you, nine times out of ten, a successful mother."[20]

Life in Utah Territory offered women and mothers plenty of opportunities to think about things outside of cooking, cleaning and changing diapers, and Martha, or "Mattie," would have a lifetime of chances to balance being a mother as well as a pioneer in medicine and politics.

Martha was born in the coastal town of Llandudno, Wales, in 1857. Latter-day Saint missionaries had great success in her native country, and Martha's family was among the many Welsh Latter-day Saint immigrants who made the long journey to Utah. Her family traveled from Liverpool, England, to New York and worked there for a time to save enough to cross the plains to Utah. Martha's infant sister died on the journey and was buried in an unmarked grave. The whole family struggled on the westward trek, and Martha's father died just three days after arriving in the Salt Lake Valley in 1861, when Martha was just five years old.

Martha's mother remarried the next year to a widower named James Paul. Paul proved to be a supportive and encouraging stepfather. Martha graduated school at age fourteen and began to teach, but the diminutive young woman had trouble keeping the bigger boys in her class under control, so she had to step down. As a new career, she learned how to set type for printing and got a job at the *Woman's Exponent*, working with two of Utah's most influential pioneer women, both writers and poets: Emmeline B. Wells and Eliza R. Snow. Martha confided in them that she would like to be a doctor, and they encouraged her in her dream, though only a handful of women anywhere in the world had achieved a medical career outside of nursing.

Then, in 1871, when Martha was sixteen, Brigham Young announced that the Utah Territory needed more doctors. Martha was galvanized. She continued to work as a typesetter during the day and took classes at night at the University of Deseret, graduating in 1878 with a chemistry degree. Brigham Young had died in 1877, but his successor as president of the Church of Jesus Christ of Latter-day Saints, John Taylor, called Martha and three other women—Ellis R. Shipp, Maggie Shipp and Romania B. Pratt—to be doctors in the Utah Territory. This meant that, to these women, their role was not just secular but was literally an assignment from God.

At eighteen years old, Martha traveled to the University of Michigan and worked while studying at one of the few medical schools that admitted women. She graduated at age twenty with her medical degree, but she was not finished with her studies. She went to the University of Pennsylvania to study pharmacy as well, the only woman in her entire class of seventy-five students. She also got a degree in oratory before returning to Salt Lake City in 1882 at age twenty-five.

Martha set up a private practice in Salt Lake City, with her stepfather providing the space, but that same year, leaders of the Church of Jesus Christ of Latter-day Saints called her to be the first resident physician at Deseret Hospital. She not only treated patients but also taught classes on nursing and obstetrics.

While working at the hospital, Martha grew close to its superintendent, Angus Cannon. He was twenty-three years older than her and a polygamist with three wives. Already, the federal government sought to punish the Latter-day Saints for polygamy and reduce the influence of the Latter-day Saints in the territory, with federal agents hunting down and imprisoning polygamists. Despite this, Martha was in love with Angus and supported the Church of Jesus Christ of Latter-day Saints in its legal troubles. She agreed to become Angus's fourth wife in 1884.

Martha's balancing act had begun. She continued her medical career and kept her marriage a secret, even from her own family, but rumors soon spread of her relationship with Angus. Giving up her position at

Many Latter-day Saint men—including Martha's husband, Angus—spent time in jail for polygamy. *Library of Congress, Prints and Photographs Division.*

the hospital, Martha fled to the "Mormon Underground" to avoid arrest. If federal officials caught her, they could force her to testify against her husband and against the many polygamist wives she knew from her work as an obstetrician—they might have hidden their marriages, but someone still had to deliver their babies.

Women on the Mormon Underground moved from one house to another, often under false names, to avoid arrest. Despite Martha's sacrifice, federal officials caught Angus and imprisoned him in 1885. Still reeling from this news, Martha found that she was pregnant with her first child. She gave birth while she was living in hiding and her husband was in prison.

Martha decided it would be better for her daughter to live in a more stable environment, so in 1886 she evaded federal authorities and fled the Utah Territory, returning to the British Isles to visit with relatives of her mother and then travel through much of Europe with other Latter-day Saints living or working abroad. While she was gone, Angus was released from jail, and he married another polygamous wife. Martha had been corresponding with Angus throughout her travels, and she responded to this news with sharp jealousy, accusing Angus of feeling only passing love for her after all she had suffered for him. She changed her address of him from "My Dear Lover" to simply "Mr. Munn," the assumed name they were communicating under.[21]

He responded, "Though you have gone through trials you believe to be cruel with fire and brimstone, you have not done so without my warmest love. You may doubt it with your whole soul, but you are loved by the man you have gone through everything for and sacrificed everything on earth for. You have been loved as much as woman has been, are and yet will be loved, as only a true heart is capable of loving you."[22]

Homesick, suffering from depression and disenchanted over her life in exile, Martha decided to return home to Utah and her husband. In 1888, she resumed practicing medicine and, along with Emmeline B. Wells, put her energy into the women's suffrage movement. Despite her less-than-ideal marriage circumstances, she also defended polygamy, arguing that it benefited women by giving them more time to devote to their own pursuits, since they did not always have to focus their attention on their husbands' needs. During her time campaigning for women's rights, she still found time for her family, raising her daughter and giving birth to a son in 1890.

Her activism did not stop with speaking about women's suffrage or with having two children to care for. Perhaps while she was cooking and washing, she was thinking about the kind of world she wanted them to grow up in and what she could do to make that happen. In 1896, when Utah became a state, women in Utah once again had the right to vote and could now hold office in Utah. Martha chose to run for a state senate seat with the Democratic Party. She was running against some prominent Republicans, including her mentor Emmeline B. Wells and her own husband, Angus Cannon. One newspaper said of the husband-wife competition, "Mrs. Mattie Hughes Cannon, his wife, is the better man of the two. Send Mrs. Cannon to the State Senate and let Mr. Cannon, as a Republican, remain at home to manage home industry."[23]

Martha defeated her husband and Emmeline to become the first woman in the United States to hold a seat in a state senate. She reported that her husband did not resent her victory. During her term of service, she put her medical knowledge to good use. In fact, this was a time when many American women leveraged the belief that women knew best about children's needs to gain political influence on issues relating to the health of women and children. Martha helped establish the state school and a hospital for the deaf and blind; presented a bill protecting working women and girls; and sponsored a law to regulate food safety. She fought lobbyists who wanted to stop examinations for medical professionals. She also spoke out against community leaders who doubted the safety of vaccines, including some leaders of the Church of Jesus Christ of Latter-day Saints.[24] This was a bold thing for a faithful Latter-day Saint woman to do and may have troubled her conscience, but her medical profession

TATE SENATOR

589 K. MATTIE HUGHES CANNON. 1899.

Senator Martha Hughes Cannon with her daughter, Mattie, in 1899. *Used by permission, Utah State Historical Society.*

was a calling, and she had to stand by what she knew to be best for the children of Utah.

Martha was pregnant with her third child during her term in office, and once her baby was born, she chose not to run again, once again making a decision balancing her family life against her professional one. Though she retired from politics, she served on the boards of the Utah State Board of Health and the Utah State School for the Deaf and Dumb. After her husband's death in 1915, she moved to California to be closer to her son, but when she died in 1932, her body was returned to be buried in the state she had served so faithfully. She had proved herself not only a successful mother but also an important influence in medicine, politics and the welfare of women and children. In 2020, Utah will honor her by sending her statue to the National Statuary Hall in the United States Capitol, one of few women represented there.

Chapter 8

THE BASSETT SISTERS

Outlaw Queens

Nothing conjures images of the Old West like bank robbers and cattle rustlers or the Range Wars. Utah might seem to be left out of this stereotype, with its mostly strict-living Latter-day Saint population, but it produced its own outlaws, and perhaps none are as colorful as the Bassett sisters. And, like all good Wild West legends, they also come with their own unsolved mysteries.

Josie and Ann Bassett, born in 1874 and 1878 in Arkansas, lived their lives literally and metaphorically on a border. Their father, Herb, bought a large cattle ranch spanning parts of Utah, Colorado and Wyoming and moved the family there. Their mother, Elizabeth, took the lead in running the ranch, a skill her daughters would inherit. Josie and Ann had a traditional eastern education at a boarding school, but they also learned the lessons of the West—how to ride horses, rope cattle, shoot and survive in a harsh environment—and the West was where they chose to live.

Josie and Ann came of age during the Range Wars, when large cattle companies fought one another and smaller ranchers for control of the open range to graze their cattle. Thanks to the railroads, there was tremendous money to be made raising cattle to be shipped to the cities, and investors from all over the United States and overseas put their money into cattle. Some of that money went into buying land or even threatening ranchers and using violence to drive the smaller companies out. Shootouts, thieving, spying and lynching were not uncommon. Smaller ranchers like the Bassetts, without big investors behind them, had to find other ways to survive.

The Pinkerton National Detective Agency's photo of Wild Bunch gang member Laura Bullion from 1901. *Library of Congress, Prints and Photographs Division.*

One of the ways they did this was by being friendly with outlaws such as Butch Cassidy's Wild Bunch. Cassidy, born Roy Parker, was a Utah-grown bank and train robber and sometime cattle rustler. The Bassetts did not ask the Wild Bunch too many questions and offered them a place to stay or to sell their "extra" cattle. In return, the Wild Bunch looked out for the Bassetts, using their quick guns to protect the smaller ranch from the hired thugs of the big cattle companies.

This close association led to friendships and even romantic relationships between the Bassett sisters and some members of the Wild Bunch. Josie and Ann were two of just five women ever admitted to Robbers Roost, the Wild Bunch's hideout. Two of those other women later married members of the gang, and one was a member of the Wild Bunch, a mixed-race woman named Laura Bullion who rode with the gang and served time in jail for train robberies. Though the sisters—and especially Ann—were quick draws and good shots themselves, their relationships with the Wild Bunch continued to protect them as they took over running their father's ranch in the 1890s with neighboring cattle companies trying to drive them off. They also led to the first mystery surrounding the Bassett sisters: did Ann Bassett live a double life as an outlaw known as Etta Place?

Etta Place was the assumed name of a mystery woman associated with the Wild Bunch. She was one of the other females said to have visited Robbers Roost, but almost nothing is known about who she actually was. She called herself Ethel in 1901 when she traveled to New York with Harry Longabaugh—the Sundance Kid—and married him. Harry was going by the name "Harry Place," using his mother's maiden name, so Etta signed her name "Mrs. Ethel Place." Harry wrote to a friend that he had married a girl from Texas, but he could have been hiding her identity, since others said Etta claimed the East Coast as home.

This might not seem to have much to do with Ann Bassett, but the Pinkerton Detective Agency, in hot pursuit of the Wild Bunch, issued descriptions of both Ann and Etta, and the descriptions are remarkably similar, including their appearance and refined language and manners suggesting a proper education on the East Coast. Modern analysts have compared photos of the two women and declared that they are almost certainly the same person. They even have the same odd mark on their hairlines, maybe a scar or cowlick. According to their findings, Etta Place was an alias used by Ann Bassett during her relationship with the Sundance Kid.[25]

And yet, the historical record throws a few shadows on this bright theory. For one, Ann was supposedly involved with Butch Cassidy at the same time the Sundance Kid was courting Etta. The men of the Wild Bunch did sometimes have relationships with the same women but not usually at the same time. More confusing still is the fact that, shortly after Etta Place fled with her husband and Butch Cassidy to Argentina, Ann Bassett was in Utah, marrying her first husband. And in 1903, Ann was arrested on charges of cattle rustling. She stood trial, but the jury could not be convinced that a woman would be a cattle rustler, so she was acquitted. While this was going on, Etta Place was, in theory, still hiding out in South America, though she and Harry made at least one visit to the United States in 1902.

Were Ann and Etta the same woman, playing some complicated legal game across international borders? Or were the two women just remarkably similar? And if not Ann Bassett, who was the mysterious Etta Place, who seems to have only existed long enough to associate with the Wild Bunch, marry one of its members and disappear with him to South America?

By the early 1900s, the Wild Bunch's glory days had ended, with most of the members dead or arrested. But Josie and Ann still had a ranch to run and cattle companies to compete with. Ann managed the family's ranch for the rest of her life. She divorced her first husband, marrying again in 1928 to fellow rancher Frank Willis, and they

Ann Bassett Willis in the early 1900s. *Denver Public Library, Western History Collection, Z-153.*

The Sundance Kid and the mysterious Etta Place in 1900. *Library of Congress, Prints and Photographs Division.*

remained devoted to each other. Even after her death in 1956, he did not have the heart to scatter her ashes.

Josie did not settle down quite so easily. In 1913, she left her father's ranch to start her own homestead in eastern Utah near Vernal. She was married five times, divorcing four husbands and burying a fifth, whom some said she poisoned. She raised a couple of sons, but after they moved away, she remained independent into her old age. She sold moonshine during Prohibition, and during the Great Depression, she often shared poached deer with starving neighbors. An enemy rancher accused her of rustling his cattle and slaughtering them, and he produced the hides on her property as evidence. She denied the charges, saying the evidence was planted, and her neighbors bailed her out of jail. Twice the case went to trial and ended in a hung jury, and finally the case was dropped. Josie continued her active outdoors life until late in 1963, at age eighty-nine, when a horse knocked her down and broke her hip. She died not long after, the last known associate of the Wild Bunch.

In her later years, Josie made a startling claim: that Butch Cassidy had visited her in the 1920s. Yet everyone knew Butch Cassidy and the Sundance Kid died in 1908. At least, men matching their descriptions were killed in a payroll robbery gone bad in Bolivia that year, and a woman fitting Etta Place's description had come looking for their death certificates. Other Utah acquaintances of Cassidy also claimed to have seen him after his 1908 death. Were they just telling tall tales, reliving the glory days of the Wild West when the sleek, modern world of the 1950s and '60s made the "olden days" seem glamorous? Or were Josie and the others offering deathbed confessions that the Wild West had lived on longer than most people supposed? DNA testing has yet to reveal the remains and resting place of Butch Cassidy or the Sundance Kid, and whatever else Josie knew about their secrets, she took to her grave.[26]

Chapter 9

CLAIRE H. FERGUSON

The Girl Deputy

Utah did not just produce early female lawmakers and lawbreakers; it also had women enforcing the law. Claire Ferguson, who would lead the way among Utah women in law enforcement, was born in 1877 in Provo, Utah. Her mother was Dr. Ellen B. Ferguson, a suffragist who worked at Deseret Hospital with other notable Utah medical women such as Dr. Ellis Shipp and Dr. Martha Hughes Cannon. Dr. Ferguson was also the first woman to serve on the Democratic National Convention.

As the daughter of a well-known Salt Lake City figure, Claire was no stranger to publicity in Utah newspapers. Much of her early publicity was in the society pages, announcing that she had gone to a house party and enjoyed cakes and music until after midnight or traveled to another city to visit friends. She was a member of the Oquirrh Club, a social club named after a local mountain range, and she was also noted as a pianist and a speaker, performing dramatic passages and songs at private parties or public gatherings.

Claire enjoyed Salt Lake City's social and political life, though she did not share her mother's medical aspirations. But Claire was an active member of the Democratic Party and the Utah Woman's Press Club, a group founded by Emmeline B. Wells and associated with the *Woman's Exponent*. The Utah Woman's Press Club's stated goals, in addition to promoting literary achievements, included encouraging education and professionalism, political activism and faith among Utah's women.

Claire attended university in Salt Lake City and then worked as a stenographer for the sheriff's office. The sheriff realized that it would be

Drawing of Claire
Ferguson from the *Salt Lake
Tribune* in 1897. *Digitized by
J. Willard Marriott Library,
University of Utah.*

useful for Claire to be a deputy sheriff so she could handle some of the
official business that could only be managed by an official deputy, such
as serving papers and summoning jurors. Claire, with her keen interest in
politics and an awareness of women's rights issues instilled by her mother,
jumped at the opportunity. She was sworn in in 1897, though there was
some concern about the legality of her appointment because she was only
twenty and deputy sheriffs were supposed to be twenty-one.[27] Nevertheless,
Claire was allowed to serve, perhaps because she was seen as a novelty.

Women on the police force were almost unheard of in the late 1800s. The
Pinkerton Detective Agency used a few female agents starting with Kate
Warne in 1856, but they were an anomaly in the law enforcement industry.
In 1891, Marie Owens of Chicago became the first policewoman in the
United States, charged with overseeing children's welfare issues. Around the
same time, a handful of women served as deputies for the U.S. Marshals.
Claire Ferguson appears to be the first deputy sheriff in the United States,
taking her place among these trailblazers in female law enforcement.

The sheriff's office was quick to assure the public that petite Claire would
not be patrolling or doing any dangerous work—it was a decade later before
a smattering of policewomen were allowed to patrol. And newspapers took
care to point out that she was still feminine. The deputy's badge, when worn
by a woman, was apparently "dainty."[28] Some articles suggested she would

use her "pleading eyes" to cajole law evaders into complying and that jurors shirking their duty and even hardened criminals would obey her quickly so they did not offend her sensibilities or force her to strain her voice—perhaps giving lawbreakers too much credit for gentlemanly behavior.

Despite these assumptions about how Claire would do her duties in "a gracious, feminine fashion," she had the same power to arrest criminals as any other deputy, and she practiced her marksmanship in case she was called on to take part in an execution, where the criminal could choose to be shot or hanged. Her "pleading eyes" were not enough to stop a mentally ill criminal from trying to escape on the way to the asylum, and she had to subdue him. They might have been more useful when she prevented a female criminal from committing suicide. Claire used her gun to apprehend the thief "Handsome" John Gray when he slipped out of the handcuffs another officer had placed on him and tried to fight his way out of police custody. Rumors claimed that she even visited Butch Cassidy's Robbers Roost, or was invited to visit, though it is not clear if this actually happened.

Much of her day-to-day work consisted of paperwork and dealing with female prisoners and truant children. In the case of Mrs. Hutchinson—a nurse who was accused of walking into someone else's home, putting on the wife's clothes and jewelry and walking out with all the valuables—Claire not only served as the stenographer for the case but was also the officer charged with escorting Mrs. Hutchinson to and from the jail and sat by her in court, comforting the woman (who seems to have had some kind of mental disorder) throughout the trial.[29]

Claire retired from her position in 1899 at age twenty-two, but she had been so valuable in her services that the sheriff replaced her with another female deputy sheriff, Kate Brockbank.[30] Claire's mother had had a falling out over the management of Deseret Hospital and, disaffected, left Utah for New York. Claire traveled with her. Claire wrote about her experiences in law enforcement for the *New York Journal* and became quite famous as "The Girl Sheriff." She also continued to be active in the Democratic Party.

In New York, Claire became the secretary for a large real estate company and then went on to work for the Yawman and Erbe manufacturing company in a "confidential capacity." It appears that Claire married lithographer Wilbur Stocker Wright in New York in 1905. She had two children, the last born in 1908. Wilbur listed her as his wife on his World War I draft registration card in 1918, when she was living in Long Island and he was working in Detroit. After that, Claire vanishes from the historical record. Her mother died in New York in 1920, and no mention is made of Claire or any of her siblings in the death notice. Claire may have died before her mother, or she might simply have retired to a quiet life, content to remember her days as the Girl Sheriff.

Despite Claire's early headway in law enforcement, it was not until 2017 that Utah had its first female sheriff, Rosie Rivera. Rosie still had to battle perceptions that women did not belong in law enforcement, but she held many positions that Claire never would have dreamed of: patrol officer, member of the Metro Gang Unit and detective. Yet some of the advice that guided Rosie could have come directly from Claire herself: work hard, stay calm and do not try to be a man; women in law enforcement have their own skills that set them apart from their male colleagues.[31]

Chapter 10

GEORGIA LATHOURIS MAGEROU

Mining Camp Grandmother

As the frontier era ended in Utah, mining camps were among the last holdouts of the Old West days and the immigrants streaming into the camps the last pioneers of that era. The miners came from all over the world: Japan, Italy, Mexico, Greece, eastern Europe and elsewhere. They were fleeing poverty or upheaval in their own countries and seeking the American dream through grueling work in Utah's mines. Many came to earn some money to send home to their families or to take home themselves, not planning on staying longer than it took to earn enough to establish their lives back home, but others hoped to find a home in America.

The immigrants in the mining camps found the American dream elusive. They worked long hours in dangerous conditions, and many died before ever seeing their homeland again. When they were not working, their homes were tents or rough wooden shacks that let in blowing sand in the summer and stinging snow in the winter. They made less than American-born workers and faced prejudice and exploitation by labor agents who made them pay bribes for their dangerous jobs and rough living quarters. The companies they worked for treated them as little more than pieces of a machine that could be easily replaced.

Most agreed that this was no place for a woman. Yet the women came, living and working alongside the men and making a place for themselves in America.

Georgia Lathouris Magerou was one of the first of these pioneering women. Born in Greece in 1860, she endured the hardships of life in a

Georgia Lathouris Mageras (Magerou) with her daughters and grandchildren. *Special Collections, J. Willard Marriott Library, the University of Utah.*

country struggling with political revolts and a failing economy. At age fourteen, Magerou, as she would later be known, was working in the fields when she heard a call for help. Another woman had gone into labor and did not have time to make it back to the village. Magerou helped the woman deliver her baby in a cave and launched herself on a lifelong career.

Magerou quickly became known for her midwife skills, and she learned folk medicine as she treated people in her village. This was fortunate because Magerou's family was very poor and could not provide her with a dowry. Without a dowry, no man in Greece would accept her as a wife.

In addition to her midwifery, she also found time to work with some foreign laborers on bridge and road construction projects near her village, and there she met an Austrian laborer named Nikos. Nikos was Catholic and a foreigner, while Magerou's family were Greek Orthodox, but he did not care about Magerou's lack of dowry. He and Magerou convinced her parents to let them marry.

Nikos and Magerou started their family, but times were still hard in southern Europe. Nikos saw the opportunities that awaited a hard worker in America, so in 1902, he set off for the foreign shores to work on the railroads and send money home to Magerou. Before long, he heard about some relatives making a good living at the mines in Utah, and he moved to what is now Magna, Utah. Once he was settled in there, he wrote for Magerou and the young children he had left behind in Greece.

When Magerou arrived in Utah in 1909, there were several thousand Greek men already living in the state but only about ten Greek women. As a forty-nine-year-old mother with nursing experience, Magerou filled the role of a matriarch to the younger people in the mining towns. The camps were filthy and crowded, without adequate housing, paved roads or sewage systems, making them breeding grounds for disease. Magerou marveled, though, at how cheap soap was in America and saw no reason to ever be dirty again. She made her home an example of cleanliness.

She also dispensed her knowledge of folk remedies to the miners. The men did not trust the company doctors, who were too quick to amputate injured arms or legs instead of trying to set broken bones. It was an easy and cheap treatment but took no regard of the well-being of the miners. A missing arm or leg disqualified them from hard labor and meant that they would quickly slide into poverty.

Magerou offered her own treatments for injuries, even serious ones the doctors did not think could be healed. She saved the legs of at least two men whom doctors said were certain to lose their limbs, and she treated many others who were sick. She did not limit herself to folk remedies, either. When she learned about the rubbing alcohol American doctors used to disinfect wounds and tools, she quickly adopted use of it herself.

Her most vital and lifesaving role, however, came as the Greek community in Utah expanded. Some of the immigrant men realized that they would be in America longer than they had planned, and they wanted to start families. Much of their money was going to support aging parents in Greece or provide dowries so their sisters could marry. They might not be appealing marriage prospects to girls who had dowries and could stay in Greece, but there were plenty of Greek women who did not have dowries and wanted to marry. Since there were almost no Greek women in Utah, the Greek men sent home for picture brides.

Picture brides married their husbands sight unseen. Their marriages were often arranged by the men in America. A man might tell his friend about the good, hardworking sister he had back home. She still did not have a dowry, but then the friend did not have much to offer either except his hard work. Then, the man would write to his sister and tell her about his hardworking friend and the opportunities in America. If the parents agreed, the wedding would be arranged, and the couple would exchange pictures, hence the term "picture bride." Sometimes the men did not send a picture of themselves, using instead a photo of a handsome American movie star like Rudolph Valentino. By the time the woman realized the picture was not accurate, she would already be in America and quickly married to her new groom, who had paid for her passage.

As women joined their husbands in the mining camps, they found themselves very alone, especially when it came time to give birth. Magerou was soon in high demand, and thanks to her skill and attention to cleanliness, she never lost a mother or child. If the birth presented difficulties, she did not hesitate to send for a doctor, but most of the women preferred to have a traditional midwife

Greek picture brides may have been disappointed to learn that their intended husbands did not actually look like actor Rudolph Valentino. Photoplay, *Volume 22, 1922.*

"Grandma Magerou" and her husband, Nikos, in the 1930s or early 1940s. *Special Collections, J. Willard Marriott Library, the University of Utah.*

deliver their babies. Magerou would also care for the women after their babies were born, making them dinner and even cleaning and braiding their hair while they adjusted to life with a new little one. The mining camps were ethnically mixed, and Magerou attended women of all races. As long as they needed her help, she would be there for them.

As the immigrant communities grew, some white Americans responded with a growing fear that the foreigners would steal their jobs. This was compounded by the fact that many of the immigrants did not understand the laws or their rights and could be tricked into working for cheaper than English-speaking Americans. Immigrants were often brought in as "scabs," or strikebreakers, when American-born workers went on strike to demand better wages and better treatment. This fear of immigrants led to a backlash of racism, manifested by blazing editorials in the newspapers, open prejudice and the appearance of the nativist Ku Klux Klan.

The KKK was known for its lynchings and violence against immigrants, Catholics, Jews, non-Anglos and anyone else it deemed not "American" enough. Its position in Utah was tenuous because the KKK also disliked the Latter-day Saint majority, but many white Utahns, including some Latter-day Saints, joined the Klan. When a group of immigrant boys ripped the white sheets from Klansmen in a parade, they revealed some prominent members of the white community.[32] This led the immigrants—and especially the women—to fear going to white doctors for help, in case they might also be members of the KKK. Magerou stepped in to fill the gap until cooler heads prevailed and the KKK faded from Utah.

As the immigrants gained more understanding of the American labor system, and as many chose to stay and make America their home, they also began to go on strike and protest against their unfair treatment at the hands of mining companies and labor agents. When they did, their wives were on hand as well, striking and protesting alongside the men. Cut off from company doctors, they continued to come to Magerou for medical help.

Magerou continued practicing medicine into her eighties. By the 1930s and '40s, Utah put more emphasis on the licensing of physicians, and Magerou did not have any formal medical training. But she still found ways to help, acting as a nurse to licensed doctors or delivering babies when doctors were too slow coming. By the time she died at age ninety, Magerou was called "Grandma Magerou" by many throughout Utah's mining communities, and she had a hand in bringing many of them safely into the world and keeping them well once they were here.

PART II

NEW FRONTIERS

In 1890, the U.S. Census Bureau declared the western frontier "closed." Railroads and telegraph lines connected the nation, Native Americans had been pushed onto reservations and even the most rugged regions had been surveyed and mapped. The country was "settled." In 1893, historian Frederick Jackson Turner suggested that it was the frontier that had made America special— that the possibilities offered by the frontier gave the United States its vigor and drive, allowing freedom and expansion and challenging the pioneers who settled it to be strong and innovative to survive. This has led to over a century of debate on the nature of the frontier and its role in American history.

Certainly by the early 1900s, the frontier era of Utah's history was rapidly coming to a close. Utah had gained statehood and put polygamy behind it. More and more, the state was drawn into the interests of the rest of the nation, including the two world wars. Technology and society were changing quickly. Western historian Wallace Stegner said of early Latter-day Saint pioneers, "That I do not accept the faith that possessed them does not mean I doubt their frequent devotion and heroism in its service. Especially their women. Their women were incredible." This could, of course, apply to non-Mormon Utah pioneer women as well. But the incredible actions of Utah women did not stop with the closing of the frontier.

Chapter 11

MAUD MAY BABCOCK

The First Lady of Utah Drama

Susa Young Gates, a daughter of Brigham Young who traveled the United States and the world advocating for women's rights, made a stop at Harvard in 1892. The prestigious Massachusetts university was already over two hundred years old, but women had only been admitted as students there since 1879, and it would not be until 1919 that Dr. Alice Hamilton became the first woman hired as part of the regular faculty. Yet the university had started a less exclusive summer school program where there were opportunities for a few outstanding women to teach courses. Susa was deeply struck by the talent of one of these instructors, a young speech and drama teacher named Maud May Babcock.

At twenty-five years old, Maud was a perfectionist with a love of learning. Born in New York in 1867, she earned her first degree from Wells College in New York, then went on to earn degrees from Philadelphia's National School of Elocution and Oratory and New York's American Academy of Dramatic Arts. Her younger brother was a surgeon, and Maud observed his operations to learn more about human anatomy and how vocal cords worked. Still, she had not learned all she wanted. She enrolled at Harvard, eventually earning the opportunity to teach in the summer school for several years.

Susa sought out Maud and spoke with her. We do not know what Susa said, but somehow she convinced Maud to strike out for Utah to seek a position at the University of Utah as a speech teacher. Maud had applied for a permanent position at Harvard, but the Massachusetts

Utah writer and women's rights activist Susa Young Gates. *George Grantham Bain Collection, Library of Congress, Prints and Photographs Division.*

institution rejected her. The University of Utah did not have any female faculty members, but the West held more opportunities for women. As a divorced mother of two returning to school, Susa had founded the Department of Music at Brigham Young Academy in 1878. And women in most western states could vote, while Massachusetts and other New

England women would not have that right until the passage of the Nineteenth Amendment in 1920. Despite the concerns of her family, Maud moved west.

Maud impressed the University of Utah faculty as well, and in 1892, she became the first female faculty member at the university. She taught not only speech but also physical education, often taking her students on hikes in the mountains. Probably thanks to her studies with her brother the surgeon, she regarded the body and mind as part of one whole, believing that it was important to "first, make the student a healthy, free animal" and that "the increased demand made upon the system by exercise of whatever character, will benefit the entire man, not a part."[33]

She approached her teaching with the philosophy that "the average student does not want to be an orator or elocutionist, but he needs expression to help him in whatever vocation of life he has chosen."[34] Regardless of their goals in life, she demanded that her students work hard. She expected them not to simply memorize passages but to know them inside and out, "without the book."

Maud wanted young people—and especially girls—to be prepared to take leadership roles later in life. She told them to learn to do more than sit still and be quiet and instead to have some "gumption." She did not let students like shy Herbert Maw slide into the background but gave him roles that would force him to stretch and grow—playing kings and jesters alike. This helped Maw to later become the governor of Utah. Others of her students were future attorneys, judges, surgeons, attorney generals, stage actors, movie stars, radio personalities and Latter-day Saint church president Joseph F. Smith. Maud said, "The aim of life should be not to make mountains out of ourselves, towering above the valleys below, but to raise the valleys."[35] Her home was always open to her students. They recognized her devotion to them and affectionately called her "Miss B."

Her passion for education and devotion to her students paid off. Maud went on to found the Department of Speech at the University of Utah, acting as its chair beginning in 1927, and also started the Department of Physical Education. She developed the university's Utah Dramatic Club, perhaps the first university drama club in the United States, and also staged what is believed to be the U.S.'s first university-sponsored play, *Eleusinia*, the first of over three hundred she would direct in her forty-six years at the school. She campaigned for years for the university to build a professional-quality theater, which was unheard of at the time. It finally relented and constructed Kingsbury Hall in 1930.

"Miss B," Maud May Babcock. *Special Collections, J. Willard Marriott Library, the University of Utah.*

Maud joined the Church of Jesus Christ of Latter-day Saints not long after her move to Utah. As a church member, she took a leadership role in the Mutual Improvement Association for young people. The church had long sought to encourage the dramatic arts in Utah, sponsoring a number of theaters and plays, and its efforts were aided by other immigrant groups that did not want to leave behind the culture they had enjoyed back east or in Europe. Maud capitalized on this interest, and in addition to her work at the university, she was involved in many community theater programs. She also advocated for the construction of the Deseret Gymnasium in Salt Lake City, which had programs for men and women, where many future athletes trained.

Maud also had a hand in developing textbooks for Utah high schools. She was disappointed by the quality of the readings in the speech textbooks. Why could the students not study the great masters of literature such as Browning, Milton and Shakespeare? Some were concerned that Shakespeare was too advanced for high school students, but Maud insisted that the students could be held to a higher standard and that they would reach the expectations with the proper guidance. She said, "There is no excuse for using inferior literature."[36]

Maud, along with Brigham Young University drama teacher Miriam Nelke and Alice Louise Reynolds, who was BYU's first Shakespeare teacher, was instrumental in training the next generation of Utahns in an appreciation of fine literature that continues today in such events as the Utah Shakespeare Festival and the proliferation of authors who hail from Utah.

Maud's dedication to education and communication went beyond the classroom and theater. She authored two books (*A Brief Introduction to Mormonism* and *What Women Should Know*), plus several textbooks and numerous articles, and she edited the *Quarterly Journal of Speech Education*. For her work, the National League of American Pen Women awarded her an honorary membership.

She continued to study, traveling to Chicago, London, Paris and China, often with students in tow. After the Sino-Japanese War broke out between China and Japan in 1937, a prelude to World War II, Maud organized relief for the Chinese people. Maud also participated on the board of the Utah School for the Deaf and Blind and eventually served as its president, as well as being president of a national drama fraternity, Theta Alpha Phi. She campaigned for female suffrage and an end to disfiguring "wasp-waist" corsets for women and started the Lucy Mack Home for Girls, meant to help female juvenile delinquents. At age sixty-nine, she became the second female president of the National Communication Association, then known as the National Association of Teachers of Speech. Adding to her list of firsts, she was the first woman in the United States to serve as a chaplain for a state senate, a post she held in Utah for twelve years.

Her personal life was as colorful as her professional one. She had a Chow Chow dog and a talking parrot from South America. She collected Chinese artifacts and dolls in authentic national costumes from around the world, which helped inspire costumes for theater productions. She liked to wear clothes in "a symphony of color."[37] Sometimes, she ran into opposition in her pursuits because of her gender or ideas that ran contrary to popular thinking, but she always stayed her course, saying, "I must stand true to myself and my work."[38]

After Maud retired from the University of Utah in 1938, she was awarded an honorary doctorate. Toward the end of her life, Maud suffered from Alzheimer's disease. She died in Salt Lake City in 1954 at age eighty-seven. Her legacy is still remembered in Utah through the Babcock Theater, the Maud May Babcock Doctoral Writing Society and the Babcock Performing Readers.

Chapter 12

ZITKÁLA-ŠÁ

Making Music for Her People

In the early 1900s, in a decision foreshadowing *Footloose* and other 1980s movies, the Bureau of Indian Affairs (BIA) banned dancing on the Ute reservation in southern Utah. They were particularly concerned about performances of the Sun Dance, a Sioux and Plains Indian ritual that had spread to other Native American nations. In the ceremony, the dancers fast and pray before days of grueling dancing, hoping to gain healing for their families and tribe. But the U.S. government wanted Native Americans to assimilate with white culture and saw the Sun Dance and other native traditions as dangerous and defiant.[39]

The Sun Dance is a sacred ceremony, not meant for public performance or detailed written descriptions. If the ritual could not be performed or repeated, it would be forgotten, which was what the Bureau of Indian Affairs wanted.

In 1913, however, the BIA met resistance from a direction it could not have anticipated: the opera stage. That year, Zitkála-Šá, a Dakota Sioux, along with Utah music teacher William F. Hanson and a group of Ute and white performers, staged *The Sun Dance*, an opera blending Sioux music and ritual with European musical traditions, to great critical acclaim.

Like her opera, Zitkála-Šá stood with her feet in two different worlds. She was born in 1876 on the Yankton Sioux Reservation in South Dakota, the daughter of a white father and a Dakota Sioux mother. In 1884, when she was eight years old, missionaries convinced her mother to send her to a government-sponsored boarding school in Wabash, Indiana. Her mother felt that free education would make up, to some degree, for the lands the government had taken from them. But the goal of this boarding school was to "civilize" Native Americans by stripping away their traditions and language and forcing them to assimilate with white culture.

Zitkála-Šá was initially excited to attend school but quickly found the experience lonely and frightening, with teachers trying to scare her into giving up her culture with threats and terrifying pictures of the devil. Instead of her Anglo name, Gertrude Simmons, Zitkála-Šá adopted her Sioux name, which means "Red Bird," but the school refused to call her anything but Gertrude. When Zitkála-Šá was able to return home, she found that she did not fit in on the reservation anymore, but she also knew she did not belong in white society.

Zitkála-Šá still loved learning and especially enjoyed studying the piano and violin. She dreamed of doing more with her life than becoming a housekeeper, as the teachers at the school expected. She began teaching music at the school and graduated in 1895, when she gave a speech on the inequality of women.

She went on to study at Earlham College in Indiana and became interested in recording the traditions of the Sioux and Dakota people and translating them into English. Zitkála-Šá started writing down the oral stories of her people. She also wrote honestly about her experiences at the boarding school. She was hired in a teaching position at Carlisle, another Indian boarding school. Richard Henry Pratt—the school's founder, who coined the phrase, "Kill the Indian to save the man"—told her that her stories were "trash."[40] Zitkála-Šá persisted, bridging the gap between native oral traditions and white written language. The *Atlantic Monthly* published many of her articles between 1900 and 1902, and she also published in *Harper's Monthly*. She was one of the first Native American women to tell her story in her own words and reached a large audience in these widely read publications. In many ways, she would spend the rest of her life translating between Native American and Anglo worlds.

Zitkála-Šá continued to study and perform music as well, and in 1900, she went to the World's Fair in Paris with the Carlisle Indian Band. After her return, she left the stifling environment of Carlisle for Boston to study music at the New England Conservatory. She also published a book, *Old Indian Legends*. It met with great success; the famous deaf-blind teacher Helen Keller even wrote to tell Zitkála-Šá how much she enjoyed the stories and to wish her luck.

The acclaim faded, though, and Zitkála-Šá had to find a way to support herself. She got a job at the Standing Rock Reservation in North and South

Music class at Carlisle Indian School about 1901. *Library of Congress, Prints and Photographs Division.*

Dakota. She was engaged to Carlos Montezuma, a Dakota physician, but at Standing Rock she met Captain Raymond Bonnin, himself one-quarter Dakota. She married Raymond in 1902 and moved with him to Utah to work with the Ute people. Their son Raymond was born in Utah in 1903.

In Utah, Zitkála-Šá continued to be interested in preserving and sharing her people's heritage. When she and her husband met music teacher William F. Hanson in Vernal, Utah, they began discussing her interest in blending Native American and European music. At first, they considered making an opera about the life of Chipeta. But perhaps in response to the banning of the Sun Dance, she decided instead to use it as the central focus of her opera. She would play the Sioux music on her violin, and Hanson helped adapt it for other European instruments as well. The Sun Dance was not meant for public performance, and Zitkála-Šá did expose some of it to the public gaze, but she kept other sacred parts of the ritual out of the opera, trying to maintain a balance between preserving and exploring her native traditions and protecting parts of her religious beliefs. The opera created a space for the Ute participants to perform their traditional songs and dances without fear of repercussions from the Bureau of Indian Affairs.

Zitkála-Šá also continued to speak up for both Native American and women's rights. In 1914, she joined the board of the Society for the American Indian, eventually becoming secretary, and wrote extensively about the need to preserve Native American culture as the editor of *American Indian Magazine.*

Zitkála-Šá. *From* American Indian Stories, *Washington, 1921.*

In 1920, women across the country were finally granted the right to vote, but Zitkála-Šá recognized that women were not yet treated equally, especially if they were Native American. Native Americans born on reservations were still not recognized as American citizens, so, male or female, their ability to vote varied by state. Most of the large Native American population in Utah did not have the right to vote. This fact came to a head during World War I, when some Native Americans were drafted despite being denied citizenship. Some, such as a group of Shoshone in Utah, organized protests against this illegal draft, but others chose to serve and try to earn their citizenship. In fact, the Choctaw Code Talkers of World War I predated the more famous Navajo Code Talkers of World War II. Upon returning from the war, these veterans could apply for citizenship individually, but their people were not granted universal citizenship.

In 1921, Zitkála-Šá joined the General Federation of Women's Clubs to continue campaigning for women's rights and to help found the Indian Welfare Committee. She, her husband and their young son had moved to Washington, D.C., to join in lobbying against these unfair practices. In 1924, they succeeded in having the Indian Citizenship Act passed. This made all Native Americans U.S. citizens but did not guarantee them the right to vote; that decision still varied by state. Zitkála-Šá and her husband helped to found the National Council of American Indians to fight for suffrage for Native Americans. Zitkála-Šá worked with the organization until her death in 1938. She was buried in Arlington National Cemetery. Shortly after her death, the New York Opera Guild performed *The Sun Dance* opera, naming it the opera of the year.

Utah became the last state to grant universal Native American suffrage in 1954, and it would not be until the 1970s that the bans on the Sun Dance and other native religious practices were lifted. But Zitkála-Šá's efforts to help white Americans understand the Native American experience paid off in other ways. In 1950, Intermountain Indian School opened in Brigham City, Utah, as a boarding school for Navajo children. Unlike Zitkála-Šá's experience, though, these youth would not be torn away from their culture. Though the Native American education system still had flaws, those like Zitkála-Šá who had spoken up about the trauma and injustice of the early boarding schools had raised public awareness and improved the educational experience of Native American students in Utah and throughout the country.

Chapter 13

KANAB'S ALL-FEMALE CITY COUNCIL

No Laughing Matter

I t started as a joke. In 1911, no one wanted to be the mayor or a city council member in Kanab, a little Utah town near the Arizona border. The job only paid a pittance, took men away from their farms and businesses and required people to make decisions that were unpopular with their independent-minded neighbors. As a prank, some young men filled the ballot with the names of Kanab women.

In many parts of the United States, women did not have the right to vote at the time and certainly not to hold office. Utah was an exception, and Martha Hughes Cannon had won a seat in the first Utah state senate in 1896, but some people still thought that women had no business thinking of anything but the management of their own homes. One anti-suffrage pamphlet said, "You do not need a ballot to clean out your sink."[41]

Nevertheless, the nine hundred or so citizens of Kanab voted the women into office, the men laughing at the stunt.

The newly elected women were not laughing, though. At first, they were offended at being the butt of a joke. But their family members supported the idea, and the local newspaper editor ran a column voicing his opinion that the women would do a great job. The women talked it over. The elected mayor, Mary Woolley Chamberlain, who was living under the assumed name of Mary Howard to protect her polygamous husband, had some political experience. In 1896, when Utah became a state, she had been elected as the state's first female county clerk. The women decided to give the people what they asked for and accepted their offices.

Kanab's all-female town council, with Mary Woolley Chamberlain in the center. *Used by permission, Utah State Historical Society.*

Mary served on Kanab's city council along with Ada Pratt Seegmiller, Tamar Stewart Hamblin, Blanche Robinson Hamblin and Luella Atkin McAllister. Mary was the oldest member of the council at forty-one and Luella the youngest at twenty-six.

To their minds, the previous male city councils had neglected many problems in Kanab. As in many small western towns, the streets were often littered with animal and household waste. There was a danger of flash floods from the surrounding red hillsides. And the town's morals were not where the women would have liked them to be. Too much frivolity occurred on Sundays, and liquor—outlawed by local "dry" laws before Prohibition struck the rest of the nation—was smuggled in too easily, leading to frequent cases of public drunkenness.

The women set about correcting each of these problems. They appointed a board of health and required livestock and domestic animals to be kept off the streets or impounded and their owners fined. Some local farmers and ranchers did not take the law seriously until their stray cows were corralled. The women sold the cows' milk while the animals were impounded, increasing the city funds, until the men grudgingly paid their fines and kept better control of their livestock in the future.

The female city council also commissioned culverts to manage storm and wastewater in the streets and required people to clean up the sidewalks in front of their houses, offering prizes for those who did the best job. To deal with the threat of floods, they had a dike built outside the town. They also laid out the town cemetery and banned slingshots, which were apparently a problem in Kanab. Sports, horse races and gambling on Sunday were also banned. Then the women set out after the bootleggers. They raised the license costs for traveling salespeople, who often brought in moonshine, and worked with the post office to prevent people from mailing liquor into the town.

Many in Kanab and in the rest of the country assumed women involved in politics would just work as instruments of their husbands. The Kanab city council women proved this was not true. The women sometimes faced tension at home with husbands or other family members who did not agree with their decisions. The women disagreed with one another at times, too, but put on a unified public face against citizens who were often outraged with their legislation. They devoted a great deal of their budget to hiring a town marshal who was willing and efficient enough to enforce some of their unpopular ordinances against the unhappy men who broke them.

Their positions were not full time and did not pay well, so the women also kept up their usual work. They managed their houses, served in church positions and continued whatever employment they had. Mary worked as a store clerk, and Tamar was a nurse. They were all married with young children. Three of the five gave birth during their terms of office, belying the anti-suffrage argument that politics would strain a woman's weaker mind and body and make her infertile. Ada alone already had six children, and her husband had to live in Salt Lake City part of the year because he served on the state legislature, leaving her essentially a single mother during that time.

When their two-year term was over, most of the women were happy to step aside from the onerous and thankless job. Mary expressed hope that more women would follow them into politics, saying women were as suited or even more suited for the role than men because they were not as distracted by business interests. Ada, perhaps smarting at the accusation that the women only won because no one else wanted the job, ran against the men in the next election and won a spot on the council again. Once her point was made, however, she also retired from politics.

Their legacy had a lasting impact, and not just on Kanab. Utah suffragettes working on the national stage, like Susa Gates Young, pointed

Suffragettes demanded the vote for all U.S. women. *Library of Congress, Prints and Photographs Division.*

to Kanab's all-female city council as proof that women were intellectually and emotionally capable, not just of voting, but also of successfully serving in political positions. In 1920, the decades of campaigning by politically minded women finally led to the ratification of the Nineteenth Amendment, giving women across the United States the right to vote.

Chapter 14

MAUD FITCH

Daredevil Hero

In 1928, the famous aviatrix Amelia Earhart made an unexpected stop in Eureka, Utah. The thirty-one-year-old pilot had already made history by being the first woman to fly across the Atlantic Ocean. She was flying cross country from California when her engine failed and she crash-landed just outside the Utah mining town, her plane nosing over and breaking a propeller. She took the crash in stride, enjoying her brief tour of Utah and meeting a kindred spirit in Eureka in a fellow female daredevil who offered her a place to stay: Utah war hero Maud Fitch.[42]

When the United States entered World War I in 1917, many young Americans were anxious to go "over there" and "do their bit." For men, their role was obvious: the United States had a very small standing army at the time, and it needed soldiers. The role for women was less clear, though. European women were serving in a variety of capacities, but the United States was in the midst of the women's rights movement and the government was uncertain if a woman's place was out on the front lines.

Women served at home by knitting wool socks for soldiers so their feet could stay dry and avoid "trench foot"; planting Victory Gardens; buying war bonds; rationing wheat, sugar and meat; or serving on local war boards to oversee the war efforts on the homefront. They also filled in for husbands, brothers and sons fighting overseas, working on farms and in factory jobs. But many women wanted to do more, especially as they fought to get the vote extended to all U.S. women. If "those who don't

Amelia Earhart in 1928. *Library of Congress, Prints and Photographs Division.*

fight, don't vote," as some anti-suffrage campaigners argued, then these women would prove that they deserved the vote by serving their country.

The army hesitated to use women's skills, doing so only when the demand for "pink-collar" jobs made it necessary. Occupations like nurse, typist and telephone operator had long been seen as suitable for women, to the extent that few if any men were trained for those "feminine" roles. Suddenly, there was an urgent need for nurses, typists and telephone operators overseas, and there was not time to train men in these skills, especially when the more pressing need was for soldiers. Many women shipped out to serve in army hospitals or as "Hello Girls" connecting telephone lines between army units.

The U.S. Navy and Marines were more forward thinking than the army and quickly opened recruiting to female volunteers, who took over stateside jobs so men were freed to go fight. The YMCA and Red Cross also brought women overseas to serve in canteens and otherwise assist soldiers behind the front lines, facing a casualty rate as high as 10 percent. But perhaps the most exciting role for Utah women overseas was that of ambulance driver.

The French and English had no hesitation using female ambulance drivers, as their manpower was greatly reduced by the war, but some American leaders questioned whether women could handle the job. They not only had to know how to drive a car—not a common skill in 1917— but also how to maintain and repair their vehicle if it broke down out in the field, under artillery fire and far from any help. Some American men, including Ernest Hemingway and Walt Disney, took their turns at the ambulance wheel, but fewer American women did. Maud Fitch, though, was not one to let convention slow her down. She was an accomplished athlete and had a reputation for racing her car around the roads of Eureka. Before the war, she had volunteered with the Catholic Church, and once war broke out, she was active in the Red Cross and other community events, like staging an "International Carnival" to promote peace and raise money for the relief effort.

Maud Fitch in uniform. *Used by permission, Utah State Historical Society.*

Maud was the thirty-five-year-old daughter of a wealthy Utah mine owner. It was her family's chauffeur who had taught her to repair her vehicle. The family's wealth would be important, as female volunteers had to pay their own way overseas for the privilege of risking their lives on the Western Front. Maud did this—not only paying her way across the ocean but also sending the money ahead to pay for her own ambulance and thirty dollars a month for her room and board. She had to take an exam on driving and maintaining a vehicle before she could go, and she was the only one in her class of twenty to pass.

When she arrived in Europe, she found that the company she was supposed to work for was poorly managed and not yet sending people out into the field. Uncertain what to do, she went to work helping refugees. She was appalled by the conditions she found there: unsanitary, crowded and with little food to go around. As a Catholic, she bonded with the French while attending Mass with them under the threat of German artillery and bombs dropped from zeppelins. Despite the dangers, she kept the people back home in her thoughts, often praying for their safety.

Maud finally found a place in the Hackett-Lowther volunteer ambulance service attached to French troops. She shuttled men from clearing stations to hospitals behind the lines but also took more dangerous jobs at the front lines. She drove through ground rutted by machinery and bombs, forests splintered past recognition and clouds of poisonous gas to rescue wounded men from both sides of the fight. German planes dropped bombs on the roads she traveled and even on the hospitals. Sometimes her ambulance stuck or broke down, and artillery shells rocked the ground as she drove near the front lines, though she joked that she could not hear them over the engine of her Ford ambulance. She had to bribe guards to drive along restricted roads and get patients to the hospital. Her shifts were often thirty hours long.

She viewed the experience as the great adventure of her generation, though she worried over the pain of the men she drove. She wrote of one experience:

> *An aviator just fell about half a mile over the fields and I had to go after him and take him back over that terrible stretch. At one time, in a potato patch, I stuck, as too many doctors had got in with him, but, with a wild prayer, I was out of the hole in only a second, and then I had to make a horrible race for the hospital, four kilometers away, and over such a road! If I jarred him he would die, and if I didn't make it in time he would die—I*

shall dream of that four kilometers all the rest of my life—but I got the poor thing there alive.[43]

For her work, the French awarded her the Croix de Guerre for heroism. She returned to the United States with no official recognition for her deeds, as was the case for most American women who served overseas. It was only after the war that army nurses were granted an officer rank (though they were still called "Miss" and paid only half of what their male equivalents earned). Hello Girls were not granted veteran status until 1978, and male and female volunteers who had driven ambulances with the American Field Service were not recognized as U.S. veterans until 1990—too late for most of them.

None of this seemed to bother Maud. She had not served for recognition. In one of her letters, she wrote, "The Americans are glorious fighters. I am so proud of them that my heart sings all the time, and their successes have aroused all my patriotism."[44] She said her efforts were nothing compared to the soldiers'.

Female World War I ambulance drivers in France with their vehicles, 1917. *George Grantham Bain Collection, Library of Congress, Prints and Photographs Division.*

She returned home to Eureka and married, but her husband died in a mining accident just two years later. Maud raised their son alone, smoking cigarettes like many women of the 1920s and continuing to race her car around the roads of Eureka. It is easy to imagine that, when Amelia Earhart showed up as her unexpected guest, the two women had a grand time speeding around the backcountry roads and sharing stories of their adventures. And when Amelia went missing in 1937, Maud likely prayed for her friend.

In later life, Maud relied on a wheelchair. This may have finally slowed her down a little, but she kept her independent spirit. When she was diagnosed with cancer at age ninety-one, she refused treatment, saying she had lived a long life and was ready to go home.[45]

Chapter 15

DOMITILA RIVERA DE MARTINEZ

A Path Home

The Mexican Revolution of 1910 turned Mexico's government on its head and rattled communities throughout the United States, especially as revolutionary general Pancho Villa raided Mexico and U.S. border towns while refugees fled north to escape. Among these were English-speaking Latter-day Saints who had settled in Mexico to escape persecution for polygamy, as well as Mexicans who had converted to the Church of Jesus Christ of Latter-day Saints and now found themselves targeted because of their religious beliefs.

Among this last group was Domitila Rivera. Growing up in Chimalhuacán, near Mexico City, she loved going to church, but their local priest did not have satisfactory answers to her many questions. Her sisters, who lived in a neighboring village, suggested that her family come and listen to "los Mormones." They did, and the family were very interested in their message, especially upon hearing the belief that the native peoples of North and South America were descended, in part, from a lost branch of Israelites and had many blessings awaiting them in the "latter days."

Domitila's mother and older sisters all joined the Church of Jesus Christ of Latter-day Saints in 1904, but Domitila was not yet eight—the minimum age for baptism. In 1907, she finally had to opportunity to join the church as well, and she dreamed of going to Salt Lake City to see the temple and participate in the highest Latter-day worship rites. The male members of her family were also interested in the message of the Latter-day Saints, but because of the hostility toward the religion in Mexico at the time, they chose not to join.

When revolution broke out in 1910, some Anglo-American Latter-day Saints who attended church with the Rivera family offered to take the children to safety in El Paso, Texas, where many Mexican Latter-day Saints had fled. Domitila's parents let the older girls go but felt that Domitila was too young. They probably would have decided differently if they knew how the revolution would affect their home. Revolutionary troops rode through the town, stealing food and abducting women and girls. Then, federal troops came through and did the same. Domitila remembered once when she and some friends ran into the woods to hide. The friends hid in the piles of fallen leaves, but Domitila climbed a high tree. From there, she watched in horror as the troops found and captured her friends, killing them when they resisted.

Her parents decided they needed a better way to hide her. They dug a deep pit in their garden, placed a thick cloth over the top of it and covered it in dirt planted with flowers, then had Domitila hide underneath in the makeshift cave. For months, Domitila lived in the darkness, her mother sneaking her food at night. Domitila was terrified to be in the dark but even more scared to come out and face the troops. Finally, her father arranged for them to sneak away to live in the mountains. They lived there for six months, and when they returned to their village, their home had been burned to the

Refugees from the Mexican Revolution in about 1914. *Library of Congress, Prints and Photographs Division.*

ground. They fled to Mexico City, and then Domitila's parents arranged for one of the older sisters to take Domitila to El Paso.

The two young women traveled north by train, though the service was slow and unreliable. At one point, they had to wait in a ruined village for weeks before another train came. They ran out of money, but kind people fed them on their journey. Domitila felt that, like the lost Israelites of the Book of Mormon, God was leading her on her path to a new home. When they reached the border, they took a bath, filled out paperwork and then crossed into the United States to meet up with their other two sisters and cousins and family members. Though there were many Mexican refugees crossing the border, the sisters had jobs waiting for them through their contacts with the American Latter-day Saints in the region. The girls saved up money to bring their mother north as well, but she was tired and homesick and died of pneumonia not long after arriving.

Domitila was homesick too, though she knew she could not go back. When some of the Latter-day Saints offered to take her to Salt Lake City in 1918, Domitila readily agreed. She worked in the home of one of the Latter-day Saint families and attended church with them. She finally got to visit the temple that she had dreamed about, and the beautiful flowers and fruit trees in Salt Lake reminded her of home. She felt at peace, and her homesickness faded. She even had the opportunity to go to school for a few months, until the Spanish influenza pandemic shut down schools and other public institutions in Utah. In 1919, Domitila's two unmarried sisters, Agustina and Dolores, joined her in Salt Lake City.

Though the sisters had friends among the white Latter-day Saints, they were still on the edges—not always understanding what was said at church and at a distance from other Mexicans in Utah. In the early 1900s, the Spanish-speaking population of Utah was still very small: only 40 individuals in 1900. A community of Nuevo Mexicanos—Spanish Americans primarily from New Mexico and southern Colorado—lived in Monticello, Utah, but the 1910 census still recorded only 166 Mexicans or Mexican Americans in Utah. By 1920, that number had grown to over 1,000, but most of the Spanish speakers in Utah were single men working in mines, on railroads or in the sugar beet fields. The majority of them were Catholic—only a handful shared the Rivera sisters' Latter-day Saint faith, and most of those were fellow refugees from Mexico. The Mexican converts were determined to find their place in their new community. Sometimes white Utahns made demeaning comments to them, but Domitila did not let that get to her, saying, "It's ignorant people who say things like that."[46]

The Rivera sisters formed the nucleus of the Mexican Latter-day Saints community, and they worked to build ties with the English-speaking Latter-day Saints and the Spanish-speaking non-Mormons in Utah. The Mexican Latter-day Saints connected with other Mexicans by setting up a grill and handing out tacos in exchange for talking to them about their beliefs.[47]

The bishop of the Rivera sisters' Latter-day Saint congregation in Salt Lake City suggested that they should minister to other Spanish speakers in Utah. Taking this suggestion to heart, the three young women traveled to northern Utah and southern Idaho, preaching the Latter-day Saint gospel to the workers in the sugar beet fields for the next year. They did not have a great deal of success, but they managed to bring a small group of Spanish speakers—mostly Mexican refugees—to Salt Lake City to join the meetings there.

Thanks to the efforts of the Rivera sisters and their fellow Mexican Latter-day Saints, the Church of Jesus Christ of Latter-day Saints recognized the small but growing Spanish-speaking membership and designated an official Rama Mexicana, or Mexican Branch, in Salt Lake City in 1922. The male leadership of the branch consisted of three men who happened to represent the background of Utah's Spanish-speaking population: one from Mexico, one from Spain and one from New Mexico. The Rivera sisters were appointed to the leadership of the Relief Society, with Domitila serving as secretary and then president. Under their direction, the Relief Society raised money to help the sick and needy and hosted dinners and shows reflecting traditional Mexican cuisine, music and dance. These not only provided comfort for Mexicans who had been forced out of their homeland but also helped the dominant white culture gain a better understanding of a rapidly growing cultural group in Utah.

As the Rama Mexicana grew, more Spanish speakers became curious about the Latter-day Saints. Two brothers, Rafael and Manuel Torres, joined the Church of Jesus Christ of Latter-day Saints in 1922. They would marry Agustina and Dolores Rivera, and Domitila also met her husband Castula Martinez through the Rama Mexicana. The group grew large enough that the Latter-day Saint leadership recognized the need for a new building for them and other congregations. As was standard practice at the time, they asked the congregations to help contribute to the costs. The Relief Society gathered, and Domitila said, "We don't have money, but we can make food to sell, and whatever we earn we will give to the building fund."[48] They raised enough money to be the first congregation to contribute toward the new building.

By the 1940s, the influence of Domitila and her sisters was expanding through their family members as well. Several of their sons and daughters

The Mexican Branch of the Church of Jesus Christ of Latter-day Saints in Salt Lake City, about 1929. *Used by permission, Utah State Historical Society.*

returned to Mexico as missionaries for the Church of Jesus Christ of Latter-day Saints. Some of their sons also served their country by fighting in World War II. The Torres brothers opened several restaurants and became well-known figures in Salt Lake City. Domitila's son Arturo Rivera Martinez served in the Korean War, performed in the Utah Opera and served as president of the Latter-day Saints' Mexico North Central Mission. Her son-in-law, Orlando Rivera, held a number of leadership roles in the Church of Jesus Christ of Latter-day Saints and in the Utah community, working with people with disabilities, helping to found the Centro de la Familia to serve Utah's children and advancing education through his roles at the University of Utah, where he started the Center for Ethnic Student Affairs and served as the associate vice president of academic affairs.

The Rama Mexicana continued to grow and be an important cultural and religious home for Spanish-speaking Latter-day Saints. It is now known as the Lucero Ward. From coming to Utah as refugees, Domitila and her sisters created a home for themselves and their fellow Spanish speakers in the Beehive State.

Chapter 16

ALMEDA PERRY BROWN

Faith and Science

Almeda Perry was born in 1878 in Lynn, Utah, in the far northwest corner of the state. Her family owned a thriving apple orchard. They worked very hard, but Almeda remembered fondly the beauty of the trees and gardens and the abundant food they always enjoyed. The other children in town often teased her because of her red hair, but she escaped by playing alone among the trees, making up stories and dreaming of travel to far-off places like New York City. Wherever life would take her, she believed that God would guide her. She took as her motto a line from Shakespeare, "There's a Divinity that shapes our ends, Rough-hew them as we will."

The first rough-hewn event in her life came when her father uprooted the family from their productive farm. He moved them to a larger plot of land near Vernal in eastern Utah because he wanted more property to leave to his sons. Hunger and poverty dogged her family's attempts to restart a successful farm. She graduated from the one-room schoolhouse in 1894 at age sixteen, but she felt trapped, saying, "There was no opportunity for further education in this frontier country and I knew there wasn't a ghost of a chance for me to go away to school"[49] because of her family's poverty. Almeda worked on her family's struggling farm and found entertainment by going to local dances, which were sometimes attended by outlaws such as members of Butch Cassidy's Wild Bunch, who were allowed in as long as they were properly dressed with hats and coats.

The same year, something even more exciting happened in Vernal: a troupe of traveling actors came to town to stage plays. Almeda remembered her childhood dreams of New York City and auditioned for a part in the theater, winning the lead female role. She was a hit with the town and with the theater troupe. The manager invited her to come along with them, promising her a career in acting.

Almeda's family objected to the plan, but she was determined to seize this chance at adventure. After her final performance, she tried to sneak away, but her two sisters and former boyfriend caught her and dragged her back to the house, keeping her locked up until the troupe was safely away from Vernal. Almeda recalled, "All night I lay wide-eyed and motionless looking into a future that seemed void of interest or purpose."[50]

The only thing left for her was teaching at the local school, and she threw her whole heart into it, trying to help the children love learning as much as she did. She agreed to marry a local man, but then he eloped with another girl to punish her for dancing with a different young man at a church dance. Almeda was crushed. Her family's home was no longer just a prison for her; it had become torture. She took what little savings she had from teaching and fled to work at a boardinghouse near Provo until she had saved enough to go to college. She chose Utah Agricultural College in Logan because it was the farthest she could get from Vernal.

Utah Agricultural College was the state's land grant college. Unlike classical liberal arts schools, land grant colleges focused on practical arts and sciences. Traditional education for women taught them refined skills useful for upper-class wives, like French, drawing, dance and public speaking. But some were starting to criticize this tendency for educated women to be nothing more than "dressed-up dolls." Land grant colleges, with their focus on the practical, offered another option by creating female-centered domestic science departments. Though this segregated women from some fields of study like engineering, it gave recognition and affirmation to the practical skills that many women already possessed in chemistry, botany and child development. It also reinforced the idea that these traditionally feminine skills had value. At a time when few colleges had female professors and some were not even open to female students, the domestic sciences provided another avenue for women to pursue an advanced education—especially if they were interested in scientific fields of study.[51]

Almeda started in the home economics program in 1897 at age nineteen. She later wrote that after "a few weeks of making little seams, hems, and patches, and of washing and ironing clothes…I decided I was not getting my money's worth."[52]

Almeda switched her major to general sciences. Not many women pursued this course, but it was one of the only other paths open to them. Almeda flourished in her math and science classes. Perhaps still longing for a place on the stage, she also took elocution. She excelled at it, and her teacher, Rosannah Canon, gave her private lessons, encouraging her to pursue the interest. One of her male math professors was horrified. "A girl with your mind settling for elocution!"[53] Though Maud May Babcock likely would have given him a tongue lashing if she'd heard his derision of the benefits of studying speech, it made Almeda think about where her life was heading. She enjoyed both public speaking and science and thought she would end up teaching one or the other. As much as she loved performing, she decided science would make a better career. Though some saw a conflict between deeply held faith and science, Almeda did not. She said, "To true scientists there is no conflict between religion and science."[54]

Almeda graduated from UAC in 1901 and got a job teaching in Logan, but she longed for something more. In 1904, she traveled well over one thousand miles by train and over rough, steep dirt roads hardly deserving the name to Colonia Juarez in Chihuahua, Mexico, just south of the U.S. state of New Mexico. Colonia Juarez was one of several colonies established in northern Mexico by members of the Church of Jesus Christ of Latter-day Saints fleeing prosecution for polygamy in the 1880s. By the early 1900s, the colonies were flourishing and needed teachers to come to their high school, providing an opportunity for Almeda to have some of the adventure she craved.

She loved living and teaching in Mexico and even convinced the administrators to allow her to stage a number of plays with the students. When her two-year contract was up, Almeda returned to Utah to teach. She also got a job working as a clerk for the U.S. Forest Service. There, she heard about the state extension program, where scientist-teachers traveled to rural areas to help people learn the best ways to improve their farms and their lives. Almeda was struck by the idea. She had lived through the struggles of rural poverty, and here was her chance to help others trapped in the same vicious cycle.

Almeda would need a graduate degree to work for the extension services, so she enrolled at the Teacher's College at Columbia University. She was finally going to New York City. Columbia itself did not admit women (and would not do so until 1983), but its teacher's college did. She thrived there and graduated in 1915, more determined than ever to help with the problems of poverty she had studied while doing her thesis research. She was troubled

Almeda Perry Brown
at her desk. 1944
Buzzer yearbook. *Used
by permission, Utah
State University Special
Collections and Archives.*

by the idea that rural children lived so close to America's food production centers, yet many of them were undernourished.

She was ready to help the children of rural Utah, but the state did not have any extension positions open. Disheartened but undeterred, she took a job teaching in Cedar City. On the train ride there, she observed her luggage sitting all by itself, and she was suddenly overwhelmed by her loneliness.

While working at Cedar City, she began corresponding with Charles Brown, who had been at Utah Agricultural College with her. He was now a widower with three young children. After many letters and several visits, Almeda married him in 1916. She was thirty-eight years old, and though she loved children and had worked with them throughout her life, she was nervous to suddenly be a mother. The Brown family settled down in Salt Lake City, and Almeda wrote, "HOME. A magical word conjuring up visions of family living with children to love and care for."[55]

For a while, their life was blissful, but then Charles lost his job. World War I broke out in 1917, and he thought his engineering degree would give him an opportunity for a defense job, but as he was forty-three, most people thought he was too old to hire. As their money ran out, Almeda looked for work as a teacher. The public schools would not hire her because they did not like married women teaching. She tried private schools, and one was ready to offer her a job until it found out she was a Latter-day Saint. Both Almeda and Charles scraped by with part-time work, with her teaching nutrition classes and him taking scattered engineering jobs.

To Almeda's surprise, she found she was pregnant in 1918. At forty, she had thought it was impossible, but she was excited. As the end of her pregnancy neared, the Spanish influenza struck Utah. The influenza killed upward of fifty million people across the globe and shut down major cities in the United States as entire families suffered and died. No family in Utah was untouched by the influenza, and the Browns were no exception. Almeda nursed her husband and three stepchildren through their illness in the last month of her pregnancy. During the ordeal, she was as hygienic as possible to avoid getting ill herself—pregnant women who caught influenza often died. Each member of Almeda's immediate family pulled through, though some of her siblings' children died. Almeda never got sick, and she gave birth to a healthy baby boy, which she regarded as a sign of the divine influence guiding her life.

World War I and the influenza epidemic came to an end, but Almeda did not know what to do with Charles. He roamed the state looking for work, but even when he found it, he did not always show up. He gambled and came home with bruises or bloody wounds from those he owed money to. He sold items from their house and wrote checks for more than they had in the bank, ruining Almeda's credit as well as his. One night, Almeda found him wandering around town with a pistol. Neither Almeda nor anyone else recognized this new Charles. At the time, doctors blamed it on his thyroid, but it is now known that some pandemic influenza survivors suffered for the rest of their lives from depression and other mental health disorders, so that might also be to blame for his altered behavior.[56]

Almeda became increasingly desperate about how to provide for her family, especially as stores refused to extend her any more credit. She had a second child but could not afford to pay the hospital bill. The hospital let her leave without paying only because it needed the bed. Almeda kept working her part-time jobs, but it was not enough. As she asked around, she heard about a new opportunity: a job with the extension office in her native Box Elder County.

Despite her other worries, Almeda was thrilled. This was the job she had trained for and longed to do. It would not only let her help other families but her own as well. In 1923, Almeda moved the children to Brigham City. There, she taught farm families about health and nutrition—advocating home gardens and the use of free-growing pioneer staples like dandelion greens to get enough vitamins—and founded the West Coast region's first Red Cross nutrition classes.[57] Her success led to an opportunity to move to Logan in 1925 to continue her research and teaching at her alma mater. It seemed a heaven-sent opportunity for her and her children, with Charles so erratic and neglectful she never knew where he was.

In 1930, Almeda got a phone call saying that Charles had been found shot in Salt Lake City. The police ruled it suicide, though Almeda remembered Charles's violent encounters over his gambling debts and always wondered if he had been murdered. It was a huge scandal, but Almeda and her friends and neighbors did their best to shelter the children from it. She decided the best thing for all of them would be a change of scene and applied to do sabbatical research at the University of California–Berkeley—the same school that had produced physicist Henry Eyring, the "Mormon Scientist" who would help convince Utahns that religion and science could coexist, as Almeda had already decided. Her lingering depression led her to seek counseling, and she immersed herself in her research, studying the nutrition in various foods to discover which would help the children of Utah be as healthy as possible. In 1933, she returned to teaching and extension work at Utah State Agricultural College.

State extension officers and professors played an important role in the Victory Garden movement. *Farm Security Administration–Office of War Information Photograph Collection, Library of Congress, Prints and Photographs Division.*

As a research scientist, Almeda had finally found her place. She published extensively about her research in nutrition and children's health, such as "Food Habits of Utah Farm Families" and "Vitamin C Content of Tomatoes." She held a position on the U.S. president's Conference on Children and as state president of the Professional Women's Club, where she fought a state law that discouraged the hiring of married women.[58] After her experience with Charles, she knew that married women were not guaranteed financial security at home. During World War II, she taught people throughout the state how to plant and grow Victory Gardens. In 1943, she became the director of nutrition research at Utah State Agricultural College, as well as the dean of the School of Home Economics.

In 1944, Almeda became the first woman to deliver Utah State University's prestigious Honor Lecture. By the time she retired in 1947, Almeda had impacted a generation of students as well as families throughout Utah through her studies, research and teaching. She moved to California and for the last twenty-two years of her life enjoyed her garden and grandchildren, feeling that the Divinity she had trusted throughout her rough-hewn life had led her to a satisfying end.

Chapter 17

MINERVA TEICHERT

Painting Stories

In the 1930s, the Great Depression held the United States in crushing agony. The stock market crash on Black Tuesday—October 29, 1929—officially started the Depression, but Utah had been suffering from a slowing economy since the end of World War I, when prices for agricultural products fell. Many Utahns lost their savings and their homes when the value of stocks plummeted and banks closed. Up to a third of Utah's male population was unable to find work, and many companies refused to hire women. They believed they should only give jobs to men who had families to provide for. A mass exodus took people out of Utah looking for work in other states.

In the midst of this dire situation, Minerva Teichert arrived in Salt Lake City in 1932. A white-haired woman in her forties who always wore a beaded headband, Minerva and her husband had a ranch in Wyoming. They had started with a rough log cabin in Idaho but worked their way up to the Wyoming house with the luxuries of running water and electricity. Now, with the Depression gripping the nation, they were in danger of losing it all. Minerva was a farm wife, but she was also an artist, telling stories of the beauty and drama of the West and her Latter-day Saint faith through her paintings. She had given up her art career for love, and now it was love that drove her to come to Salt Lake City in the hopes of saving her family's home. She approached an art dealer, Alice Merrill Horne, and unrolled a mural she had painted in the living room of her home. Alice studied the painting in amazement and immediately agreed to help Minerva. She arranged for a showing at a local gallery. Soon, the two

Minerva Teichert, *far left*, with some of her family. She is wearing her signature headband. *Special Collections, J. Willard Marriott Library, the University of Utah.*

women had sold enough murals to save the Teichert ranch, and Minerva launched a new career.

Minerva had decided she was an artist at age four, when her mother gave her a set of watercolor paints. Born in Ogden, Utah, in 1888, Minerva later said, "My parents were dreamers."[59] Her father had run away from home in Boston to go west, and her mother was the daughter of Latter-day Saint vigilante and outlaw Wild Bill Hickman. When Minerva was very young, her parents moved her and her nine siblings to a remote homestead in Idaho. Minerva worked on the ranch along with her family and was deeply impressed by the beauty of the western landscape. She often spent her spare time studying nature and people and sketching the scenes around her. Though she was too far from any settlement for formal education, her father had come from a cultured background, and both of her parents appreciated learning. They taught her geography, history and literature, including scriptures and the works of William Shakespeare.

In 1902, when she was fourteen, Minerva left home to work as a nursemaid in San Francisco. While there, she visited art museums and took classes at the Mark Hopkins Art School. She returned to Idaho to graduate from Pocatello High School and get a teaching job so she could save money to go east and study her passion. She said, "I *must* paint. It's a disease."[60] She was finally able to attend the Art Institute of Chicago. The students and professors there teased her by calling her Miss Idaho, and she felt that her professors were unfairly hard on her work. When she confronted one of them about it, he told her he demanded more of her than the other students because he saw more potential in her work.

She had to take breaks from her education to earn more money, but she persisted and graduated in 1912. She felt there was still more that she needed to learn about art. She returned to Idaho again to teach and farm while saving money, living on a homestead of her own where she always kept a pistol under her pillow. Two young men courted her during this time in Idaho, including Herman Teichert, a ranch hand and the son of German immigrants. Both of their parents objected to their courtship because they came from different religions, and Minerva's mother offered to pay for her to leave Idaho and continue her education. Minerva agreed.

She entered the Art Students League of New York City, an important art school at the time. She excelled there and earned a scholarship. Her mentor, Robert Henri, declared her one of his top three students. He also encouraged her to embrace her religious and western roots—to tell the stories she knew and loved best and felt called to paint. While studying in New York, she developed her distinctive style, using colors inspired by the western landscape highlighted with red. Newspapers in Utah and Idaho ran stories about her successes in the Big Apple. Between her studies, she still worked to earn her keep, sketching cadavers for medical schools, illustrating children's books and performing rope tricks and Native American dances that she had learned on her parents' homestead near the Fort Hall Reservation. She was also involved in women's suffrage meetings, having gone from the freedom of the West to the more restrictive politics of the East.

Minerva loved New York, and her professors believed she was poised to become a great success in the art world. But amid all her successes, her thoughts kept returning to Herman. She chose to turn her back on the glamour of New York and returned home to Idaho.

She and Herman married in 1917. Shortly after their marriage, he left to fight in World War I. Minerva continued her painting, drawing inspiration from the landscapes and stories of the West. When she did not have enough money for art supplies, she would draw on wood or paper scraps. She gave birth to her first child while her husband was fighting in the war. In 1918, Minerva and her infant caught the Spanish influenza that killed millions around the globe. As she came near to dying, she thought of how she had not had the chance to paint the stories she wanted to tell and promised God that, if she lived, she would use her talent in His service. She and her infant recovered, though her hair began turning white after her fight with influenza.

Despite her difficulties and her distance from any artistic community, she persisted in her art. Herman survived the war, and the couple eventually had five children. Minerva was happy on their ranch, working hard all day to cook for her family and the ranch hands, feeding animals, washing, cleaning and sewing. Always, in a brief moment between chores or after her children were in bed, she continued to paint. While she worked, she would tell her family members and visitors the stories behind the paintings, whether they were of animals, Native Americans or scenes from the Bible or Book of Mormon. Her work was about more than light and colors—those were just tools to tell those stories she loved.

She tried to use her talents to help others as well. She painted wedding and funeral bouquets as keepsakes for families and taught art to neighbor children, as well as keeping her door open to those in need. She may have thought that was the end of her calling as an artist, but the struggles of the Great Depression opened new doors to her.

Though it was financial desperation that drove Minerva to Utah to sell her work, she did it at the right time. Large murals like those she specialized in were popular as public art displayed where anyone could enjoy them, even those struggling with hunger and hopelessness. With Alice's help, Minerva's paintings gained an audience, and her western- and Latter-day Saint–themed art became popular in Utah. She had walked away from her art career in New York, but it had found her again.

During her career, Minerva painted over four hundred murals. The Church of Jesus Christ of Latter-day Saints hired her to work in the Montpelier, Idaho tabernacle and the Manti, Utah temple—the first woman to paint murals for these important buildings. She was able to sell several of her works to Brigham Young University to help some of her family members and neighbors' children attend college there. In 1947, she won the church's Centennial Art Contest.

Trends in art were beginning to change in the late 1940s, though. Murals like Minerva's fell out of favor, and she found it more difficult to sell her

Mormon Trail Hand Cart Train by Minerva Teichert. *Used by permission, Utah State Historical Society.*

work. Also, Alice Horne, her longtime friend and business partner, passed away in 1948, and Minerva did not have the connections the art dealer did. Minerva began having trouble selling her paintings. She took many of her religious paintings to the Church of Jesus Christ of Latter-day Saints, but it turned them down, preferring a different style. She was able to sell some of her Western paintings, but the heyday of her career was over. When a granddaughter asked her if she was famous, she smiled and replied, "No, but I will be someday."[61]

Minerva continued painting, driven to tell stories through art even if no one seemed to be listening. Her career came to a stop when she fell and broke her hip, possibly because of a stroke. Her eyesight had already begun failing, and she experienced lead poisoning from her paints. She died in 1976 in Provo, Utah.

But her prediction to her granddaughter came true. Her art has enjoyed a resurgence in popularity as new generations view the stories that she wanted to share with them. Her works are now displayed across Utah and the West and are frequently reprinted in Latter-day Saint publications.

Chapter 18

KUNIKO MURAMATSU TERASAWA

Voice of the Japanese in World War II

On December 7, 1941, Japanese planes attacked the U.S. Navy ships stationed at Pearl Harbor, Hawaii. The surprise attack rocked the nation and propelled the previously neutral United States into World War II. American men rushed to enlist in the armed forces, while American women prepared to take over many of the factory and agricultural jobs the men left behind.

In this frenzy of patriotism, many American citizens of Japanese descent also wanted to serve their country, but when they showed up at recruiting stations, the military turned them away. There were many Japanese American men in the Hawaii Army National Guard who had helped maintain order after the attacks on Pearl Harbor, but soon they had their weapons stripped away and were expelled from the National Guard.

This was only a preview of the fear and prejudice Japanese Americans would face during the war. It was especially confusing for the Issei: American residents who had been born in Japan and were denied citizenship because of their heritage. They were no longer Japanese but were not allowed to become Americans, leaving them in limbo. To make matters worse, the government shut down Japanese-language newspapers, arrested Japanese community leaders and forced all West Coast Japanese Americans into prison camps as potential spies and saboteurs. With their newspapers banned and their community leaders gone, Japanese Americans did not know about new laws that affected them like curfews or who to turn to for information they could trust. An Issei woman in Utah, Kuniko Muramatsu

Japanese nationals and Japanese Americans from the West Coast were moved to relocation centers like this one during World War II. The Utah camp, called Topaz, was near Delta, Utah. *Farm Security Administration–Office of War Information Photograph Collection, Library of Congress, Prints and Photographs Division.*

Terasawa, would become an essential link in the Japanese American community during the war.

Kuniko was born in the Nagano prefecture in Japan in 1896. She was an excellent seamstress and taught embroidery in Japan. In 1921, she met Uneo Terasawa, who had emigrated from the Nagano prefecture to America and then returned to Japan to find a wife. He had lived in San Francisco and worked for the *Shin Sekai* newspaper there before moving to Utah. Utah already had a small but thriving Japanese American community, established by railroad workers who had migrated to Utah and increased by farmers who were famous for their celery and strawberries. Utah even had a Japanese-language newspaper, the *Rocky Mountain Times*. The *Rocky Mountain Times* had a Christian focus, however, and Uneo and many other Japanese were Buddhists. In addition to farming, Uneo started a newspaper with a Buddhist perspective, the *Utah Nippo*, and was a leader in the Japanese American community. Kuniko agreed to join him in America.

Once in Utah, they worked together to support the Japanese community there. They helped raise money for a Buddhist temple and bought out the *Rocky Mountain Times*, merging the two papers and serving a wider audience, with articles in both Japanese and English. The couple had two daughters who were Nissei, or first-generation American-born Japanese.

Then, in 1939, Uneo caught pneumonia and died. Left a widow with two young children, Kuniko considered what to do. Running the newspaper was difficult and time-consuming, but if she let it die, the Japanese speakers in Utah would not have a source of information and all the people working for the paper would lose their jobs. She could not let that happen, so she continued the *Utah Nippo*, working as a reporter, editor, typesetter and publisher.

After Pearl Harbor, the *Nippo* published two editions of the paper, reporting on national and international news to the Japanese American community of Utah. On December 11, 1941, the U.S. government shut down Kuniko's paper and arrested many Japanese community leaders in Utah. Kuniko waited to see if she would be arrested as well, but the authorities never came for her. Still, her voice had been silenced, and she watched as her fellow Japanese-speaking Utahns lived in fear and confusion, with government officials taking away guns, radios and even cameras and new laws were passed prohibiting them from buying land. At the same time, the Topaz prison camp opened near Delta, Utah, for some of the Japanese Americans removed from the West Coast.

Recognizing the need to get information to the confused Japanese-speaking members of the community, in February 1942, the government allowed Kuniko to resume printing the *Utah Nippo*—one of only three Japanese-language newspapers allowed in the United States. As a result, her circulation grew to ten thousand subscribers all across the country, and she had a responsibility to keep them informed. The paper was only supposed to reprint articles found in English-language newspapers, though it did sometimes run articles by Japanese speakers, including those who were in the camps. Each edition had to pass through censors before it could be published. Kuniko worked closely with the Japanese American Citizens League (JACL), an organization dedicated to combating prejudice and misunderstandings about Japanese Americans and securing their rights. The JACL and Kuniko promoted a message of patriotism and not "rocking the boat," which they hoped would help the Japanese community survive the wartime anti-Japanese hysteria.

After the war, the government loosened the restrictions on Japanese newspapers. Kuniko's circulation dropped, but she kept publishing. She

Kuniko Teresawa (*center*) with former World War II internment camp prisoner Henry Kasai (*right*), who was a leader in the Japanese community along with his wife, Alice Kasai. *Special Collections, J. Willard Marriott Library, the University of Utah.*

continued to be concerned about the welfare of her community, especially the Japanese-speaking Issei. She said, "Money is not important. People are."[62] She established sister city status between Salt Lake City and Matsumoto, Japan, and worked for better understanding between both nations. Japanese consuls visiting America consulted her, and she became well known in both countries for her work. One of her daughters went on to teach at the University of Utah, while the other helped her mother run the paper. In 1966, Salt Lake City tore down the traditional Japantown, including Kuniko's offices, to build the Sports Palace. She considered stopping publication of the paper, which by then served around one thousand subscribers, but she decided to move to a new location, along with all of her antique equipment, and continue publishing because "old things bring much joy. As long as I'm breathing, this is what I want to do."

For her dedication, Kuniko won Japan's Order of the Sacred Treasure, "Zuihosho—Fifth Class." It was presented to her by Judge Raymond Uno, who had been incarcerated in a prison camp during World War II and then volunteered with the U.S. Army, eventually going on to become

Utah's first ethnic minority judge. In 1987, Kuniko was also awarded the Million Yen award from the Avon Josei Bunka Center in Japan, and she immediately turned the award into scholarships funds at the University of Utah. She was recognized for her lifetime of service by the JACL and earned a feature in AARP's *Modern Maturity* magazine for her ongoing service well into her golden years.

Even in her nineties, she continued hand-setting the antique type for the *Nippo*. The paper did not come out every day anymore, and fewer modern Japanese speakers could read the old style of font that she used, but she wanted to keep the tradition alive, and she enjoyed doing it. She worked until her death in 1991 at age ninety-five. Her daughter donated the complete collection of the *Utah Nippo* to archives and libraries in Japan and Utah, sharing Kuniko's life work, and a record of many decades of Japanese American life, with both of the communities that Kuniko loved and served.

Chapter 19

MARJORIE REDDING CHRISTIANSEN

Fly Like a WASP

In the 1970s, the U.S. Air Force announced it was going to do something revolutionary: allow women to attend flight school. It was, they said, the first time women would fly for the U.S. military.

But they were wrong.

Marjorie Redding Christiansen was one of several hundred women who were galvanized by the U.S. Air Force's announcement. They petitioned Congress to finally be recognized and remembered for their service to their country decades earlier during World War II when they had flown planes for the army. They spoke for over one thousand female pilots, many of whom had passed away, some in the line of duty. These female pilots had been forgotten by their country and the history books, but they decided the time had come to tell their stories.

Marjorie Redding was born on a homestead in Montana in 1920. Her family moved to South Dakota, and there she went to college to be a teacher, excelling in math and science. During her final year of schooling, in 1940, she heard about the Civilian Pilot Training Program, designed by the government to train more civilian pilots across the country. With World War II already ravaging Europe, there were also thoughts about the military value of having more pilots ready to go to war if necessary. All interested men and women could attend ground school, but only those with the top scores would be allowed to fly, and only one female would be admitted for every nine males. It was this same program at the Tuskegee University in Alabama that produced the Tuskegee Airmen—the first

African American pilots in the U.S. military—and it would break new ground for female pilots as well.

Marjorie was already editor in chief of the school yearbook and busy with her final classes, but she was drawn by the idea of learning to fly, so she found time for ground school. There were almost as many women as men in the program, but so few of them would be allowed to go on to flight training that her chances were very small. Still, the topics they learned in ground school—like aeronautics, navigation and weather—fit with Marjorie's interest in math and science, and she excelled. She later said, "I was the lucky girl." She was selected to move on to flight school.[63]

Flight school meant getting up before dawn for flying lessons, taking off and landing from grass fields and practicing dangerous maneuvers like recovering from a stall so she would be ready if it happened outside of training. Then Marjorie would hurry back to teach a college class and work on her own studies, with a little time left to apply for jobs after she graduated. When she graduated from college in 1941, it was under a looming shadow of fear over what would happen to the world if Nazi Germany won the war.

Like many women, Marjorie stepped into traditionally male roles after the United States entered the war that December and the bulk of the young men left to fight. She got a job teaching high school, and when the school day was over, she hurried over to work in an aircraft factory in Wichita, where she was the final inspector ensuring that the aircraft were built correctly. She also flew with the Civil Air Patrol, which the U.S. government authorized in December 1941 to supplement the efforts of the Air Force in patrolling U.S. air space.

In 1943, Marjorie heard about another way to serve her country. The military was experimenting with training female pilots to see if they were able to handle military planes and take over domestic flight duties so male pilots could leave for combat. At age twenty-three, Marjorie went to Texas to enlist in the Women's Air Service Pilots (WASPs). Twenty-five thousand women applied, but fewer than two thousand were accepted, and Marjorie was one of them. Of the one hundred women who entered the program in her class, only fifty-seven—including Marjorie—graduated and went on to fly military planes.

As a WASP pilot, Marjorie had a variety of jobs, from shuttling military planes and commanders around the country to testing planes that had been brought in for repair. Marjorie's experience working in the aircraft factory served her well in that role. Marjorie once spotted a plane that had been wired backward, so the controls would have moved the plane the opposite

Women Airforce Service Pilots in World War II. *U.S. Air Force photo.*

of the direction the pilot steered, but her supervisors were reluctant to acknowledge the mistake. Luckily, she convinced them she was right before another unfortunate pilot took the plane into the air.[64]

The WASPs tested out the new B-26 Widowmaker plane and would fly while hauling targets behind them so male pilots could practice shooting live ammo. Thirty-eight women died as part of the WASP program. Because they were considered volunteers and not official military pilots, the military did not pay for their burial services, but their fellow WASPs banded together to pay for the funerals, often placing flags on their coffins. This was technically not allowed because they were not enlisted, but the women felt the fallen WASPs had earned the honor.

When the war was over, the military dismissed the WASP pilots. Commercial airlines were not interested in hiring female pilots except as flight attendants, so Marjorie decided to work as an air traffic controller. She trained in California and then came to Utah to work. She was nervous about going to Utah because she had heard rumors about polygamy and that Mormons had horns, but she fell in love with Utah once she arrived.

She also fell in love with her boss, Raymond J. Christiansen, and they were married. Since she could not be married to her boss, she had to retire from the air traffic controller job, but she stayed in Utah and joined the Church of Jesus Christ of Latter-day Saints. She raised six children and became interested in genealogy, training others to research their family history. Marjorie also became actively involved in the Boy Scouts of America. She helped found the Cub Scout group in the Enoch-Parowan area and eventually became the area director.

Marjorie was awarded the Second Miler Award and Silver Beaver Award by the Boy Scouts of America, as well as being recognized by the Arnold Air Society/Silver Wings project with Wings Across America. It took until 1977 for Marjorie and the other WASPs to be granted official veteran status, and this was done only after they had petitioned Congress for recognition. By that time, fewer than 300 of the 1,074 WASPs were still alive. Marjorie died at age eighty-eight in 2008 in Goshen, Utah. She was posthumously inducted into the South Dakota Aviation Hall of Fame and awarded a Congressional Gold Medal recognizing her service to her country.

The work of Marjorie and other WASP pilots proved that women could handle military aircraft and serve with as much courage and intelligence as men. Though their contributions were largely forgotten for many decades, the WASPs inspired other women and paved the way for later female pilots in military aviation and the space program.

Chapter 20

MIGNON BARKER RICHMOND

Lifting Utah's Children

Mignon Barker Richmond's life work was helping children, but she fought a hard battle to be allowed to do it.

Mignon was born in Salt Lake City in 1897 to parents who worked at a local hotel. Her father, William, had been a slave who ran away to join the Union army in the Civil War, and her mother, Mary, was a white immigrant from London. Marriage between blacks and whites was illegal in Utah, and mixed-race children were subject to a great deal of prejudice, but her hardships gave Mignon a sympathy for people of all races.

Mary was actively involved in the Calvary Missionary Baptist Church. This church started in the late 1800s when a group of black women in Salt Lake City began to meet for a prayer group in their homes. By 1892, the group was large enough to found the Calvary Baptist Church, which opened its doors to people of all races. Mary instilled faith and determination in her daughter, which would serve her well throughout her life.

By the age of thirteen, Mignon was working as a housekeeper to save money for college while attending high school. In 1917, when she finished high school, no African American had ever graduated from a Utah college. Mignon enrolled in the Utah State Agricultural College (now Utah State University), studying home economics, textiles and foods. She took an active part in college life, becoming secretary and treasurer of the Empyrean Club, a group for writers, and joining the Turnverein athletic club. She had many white friends on campus but also faced prejudice. One professor said a

Mignon Barker (*top left*) as a member of the Empyrean Club, 1921 *Buzzer* yearbook. *Used by permission, Utah State University Special Collections and Archives.*

"Negro" would never earn better than a C grade, and some professors held back her diploma and delayed her graduation.[65] Mignon persevered and earned her bachelor's degree in 1921 at age twenty-four, Utah's first African American college graduate.

Just having her degree was not enough to earn Mignon respect. She had to search for a year and a half to find work, and when she did, it was in the University of Utah Home Economics Department—as a maid. She married once in 1925, but the relationship did not last. She continued to work odd jobs and volunteer in the community. In 1933, she married Thomas Richmond, who had a daughter from a previous marriage. Mignon was thrilled to adopt the child. She never had children of her own, but she was a mother to all the children in her life.

It was the outbreak of World War II that finally gave Mignon an opportunity to step onto the larger stage. The shortage of workers meant that employers were more open to hiring women and people of color. Mignon got a job supervising youth who were volunteering with the United Service Organizations (USO), which provided entertainment and support for the troops. She also found time to volunteer with the YMCA, the Red Cross and LDS Hospital.

In 1948, Mignon finally had an opportunity to work in the field she had studied when she was hired to start the first school lunch program in Utah at the Stewart School. This helped students whose parents struggled to provide their families with enough food to get at least one healthy meal during the day. She developed classes for the Utah State Industrial School for troubled youth and in 1957 became the Salt Lake City YWCA food services director. When she traveled by train with other YMCA leaders to Washington, D.C., though, she had to sit apart from them in the blacks-only car. Despite these ongoing prejudices, she maintained a sense of humor, patience and forgiveness and a desire to help others.

Wanting to help African American children, she served with the NAACP and helped to found the Nettie Gregory Center in Salt Lake City, which offered a safe place for black youth and other young people to gather for recreation and social activities. In 1962, at age sixty-five, she retired from her job, but her work did not end there. She became the head of the Women's Job Corps and Project Medicare Alert to help seniors. She also volunteered with the VISTA program tutoring children and started a program to teach Latino children good nutrition. Her concern for youth and seniors of all races led her to campaign for anti-poverty legislation through the Utah Community Service Council and the Women's Legislative Council and to work with Calvary Baptist Church to sponsor youth programs and affordable housing for seniors.

Mignon's effects on people of all ages and races in Utah can be seen by the variety of groups that honored her during her lifetime—the NAACP, the National Council of Jewish Women, the Young Women's Christian Association, the Salt Lake Council of Women and the Community Services Council—as well as her receipt of the Outstanding Senior Citizens Award.

Mignon died in 1984 at age eighty-six. After her death, the Richmond Park in Salt Lake City was created in her honor, and Utah State University started the Mignon B. Richmond Society to support multicultural students. More important than these honors and awards, however, were the many lives she touched through her lifetime of service.

PART III

BEYOND FRONTIERS

Utah had been the misfit of the United States in the early 1900s, with its history of polygamy and the visible role played by its dominant religion. But the state's roles in World Wars I and II proved its patriotism, and the presence of many defense-related industries as well as Hill Air Force Base solidified Utah's ties to the rest of the country. National events like the civil rights movement and growing concerns over international wars and the environment would affect Utah along with the rest of America. Many Utah women drew from their experiences of the past to reach through the social, political and religious barriers causing divisions in Utah, helping to bring healing and change to the state, the nation and sometimes even the world.

Chapter 21

RUEY HAZLET WIESLEY

Growing Peace

In 1939, fear loomed over the United States and the world. World War II had started in Europe, and many adults in the United States still remembered the gruesome horrors of World War I, the men returning with shell shock or missing limbs. With Nazi Germany expanding and the Allied powers rallying against them, it seemed only a matter of time before the United States went to war again.

Ruey Wiesley had these concerns on her mind when she visited the newly rededicated American Legion Peace Gardens—or Peace Garden of the Nations—in Cleveland, Ohio. The large park was created by veterans of World War I to promote peace and understanding. The Peace Garden is made up of smaller gardens created by various immigrant groups representing the cultural achievements of their home nations, as well as a shrine holding intermingled soil from around the world with the words "In America, peace, understanding, amity, and cooperation among peoples of all nations."[66]

The idea struck Ruey. It seemed to her that such a message of peace and harmony was needed in the world, and she returned to her home in Salt Lake City with a new dream to start such a garden in Utah.

Born in Iowa in 1886, Ruey had worked as a teacher until her marriage to Otto Wiesley in 1910. They moved to Wyoming and then Utah, where Ruey was a librarian and dean of girls, as well as a Boy Scouts leader. Otto and Ruey were both members of the American Legion, a veterans' association, and Ruey held a position on the Salt Lake City Council of Women, where women on the boards of various Salt Lake City volunteer organizations could meet together to discuss common goals and concerns. Ruey had already proposed a suggestion to have the American flag displayed at all polling places during voting. Now, she approached the other women with the idea of founding the Salt Lake City International Peace Gardens.

The Council of Women was excited by her suggestion and agreed to go forward with the project. The group elected Ruey president in 1941 with this goal in mind, but the bombing of Pearl Harbor on December 7 launched their civic efforts in a whole new direction as the United States entered World War II.

Ruey told the Council of Women, "When democracy is at its tottering point, when the moral fiber of a nation is frayed at its edges, it is the housewife, the mother, the homebuilder, who replenishes the world with the strength of purpose and thought needed for such a battle."[67] She led wartime service efforts with the American Red Cross and at Bushnell Military Hospital in Brigham City, where the U.S. Army treated thousands of wounded soldiers. In 1942, she was elected chairwoman of the Women's Division of the War Finance Committee in charge of selling bonds to help finance the war effort. She spent upward of six thousand hours on the war bond drives and traveled over thirty thousand miles through the state of Utah organizing county committees to help sell war bonds. Her committee sold $37 million in bonds—worth nearly $600 million in today's dollars— earning commendations from the federal government for its efforts.

When the war ended, Ruey's thoughts again turned to peace. Now more than ever, the state and the world needed reconciliation and understanding. Once again, Ruey recalled her dreams of the International Peace Garden and returned to her goal of organizing one for Utah. The year 1947 would be the centennial of the Mormon pioneers reaching Utah, and it seemed like a good goal to have the gardens dedicated in time for the celebration.

The Council of Women obtained eleven acres of land along the Jordan River from Salt Lake City. Ruey divided the gardens into sections, with the goal of having various ethnic groups living in Utah take different sections of the garden and design each according to their own tradition.

The Council of Women designed the "American" gardens first. For the second section, they thought it appropriate to have a Japanese garden as a symbol of healing between the two nations and between the white and Japanese populations of Utah, whose relations were strained after the wartime anti-Japanese prejudice. They asked Henry and Alice Kasai to oversee the Japanese gardens.[68] Henry had been incarcerated during the war, and Alice had become president of the Salt Lake chapter of the Japanese American

Right: Ruey Hazlet Wiesley inspecting plants for the International Peace Gardens. *Used by permission, Utah State Historical Society.*

Below: Dedication plaque for the Salt Lake City International Peace Gardens. *Photo by author.*

Citizens League, which advocated for Japanese rights and Japanese families during the war. Japan donated one thousand cherry trees for the garden, but U.S. Customs burned them when they arrived in the country. Utah citizens raised money to replace them, and Japan also sent replacement trees, helping to strengthen ties between the communities.[69]

These first two garden sections were officially dedicated in 1952. More sections were added over the years for Denmark, Holland, Sweden, Scotland, Greece, China, Finland, England, Switzerland, Italy, Lebanon, India, Wales, Canada, Norway, Africa, Brazil, the Philippines, Germany, Mexico, Korea, Russia, Ireland, Vietnam, France and Tonga. Utah immigrants designed each section of the garden. More groups were interested in adding sections, but the gardens ran out of space.

Ruey continued to oversee the gardens until her death in 1968, and the Salt Lake Council of Women still manages them. With her dream fulfilled, Ruey continued to be involved in her community, such as holding dinners at her house for college students who could not go home for holidays. Even in small acts, she reached out to include others, leaving a legacy of peace and beauty for Utah.

Chapter 22

ALENE DALTON

The Story Princess

Alene Dalton wore ball gowns and tiaras and played a character named Princess Summerfall Winterspring on a children's TV show, but beneath the tulle and sequins, she had a brilliant understanding of business and child psychology.

Alene Olsen was born in Brigham City in 1915. She studied at the University of Utah and earned a bachelor's degree in child psychology, then found work as a teacher. She was disheartened to discover that there were not any bright, cheerful children's songbooks available for her classroom, but her upbeat personality kept the children engaged in the other activities she used to teach them.

In 1938, Alene married Ross Dalton in Salt Lake City. Ross had studied at the influential theater school at the Pasadena Playhouse in California and then returned home to Utah, and his expertise would prove helpful to the couple. Alene loved being around young people but did not have any children of her own. She said, "I think that wherever there are children—and I can work with them—that's Utopia as far as I'm concerned."[70]

She left teaching to open a nursery school in her basement. The school was very successful and quickly outgrew her home. By the outbreak of World War II, she had three hundred children in her care. She often composed rhymes and songs to teach to the students. One of her songs, "Mom Says Not to Worry," became a national hit.

World War II was very stressful on families and children, with fathers and older brothers fighting overseas, the radio bringing little news or comfort and

Alene Dalton as the Story Princess, 1952. *Used by permission, Utah State Historical Society.*

families always on the lookout for the dreaded telegram telling them a loved one was missing or had been killed. Alene sensed the stress in her young charges and wanted to do something to ease their anxiety. Remembering her desire for a cheerful songbook for children, she wrote some upbeat rhymes and asked a friend, Myriel Ashton, to compose melodies to go with them. She enlisted another friend, Erla Young, to create illustrations so they could turn their songs into a book for children. Myriel and Erla both had husbands fighting in the war and young children at home, and they were grateful for the project to distract them from their worries.[71]

By the time they finished their book, the war was coming to an end and there was a national paper shortage. Publishers were not sure there was really a demand for a children's songbook, but the three friends felt their book was still important and would help children. They gathered up enough gas ration stamps to make the drive to Chicago to talk to the publishers personally. The publishers would not risk publishing a book that might fail, so they agreed to publish the book only if the women could get five thousand preorders for it.

Undaunted, the three friends set off on a road trip with Erla and Myriel's children to sing the songs in classrooms across the country. The songs and the book were a hit with students and teachers, and by 1947, the book was in print as *My Picture Book of Song*. As Alene predicted, the book was in high demand by teachers who wanted just such an upbeat songbook.

Alene's natural rapport with children and creativity and skill at entertaining them led to another opportunity for her: in 1946, she got a spot on a local radio program where she read fairy tales and other stories to children. In 1949, this led to a weekly TV show on KSL's Salt Lake City station, where she created the Story Princess persona. Her husband, drawing on his theater background, produced and directed the show, and she wrote the episodes. She began by singing, "Fairy tales can come true. It can happen to you,"[72] and she told stories, taught songs and crafts, entertained celebrity guests and sponsored a "Think Kind Thoughts, Do Kind Deeds" club. Children would write in to her telling about kind things they had done, and she would induct them into the club on the air.

Critics found her show "enchanting," and the Story Princess soon gained national attention. In 1953, she and her husband took her show to New York, and it was picked up by ABC. The show ran until 1960. Alene made appearances on *The Kate Smith Show* and *The Perry Como Show* and created the first ninety-minute TV spectacular for children. She had a regular spot on the *Howdy Doody Show*, where she played Princess Summerfall Winterspring and the character of Heidi Doody. Her performances won awards for best dramatic show in the nation, best radio show for children, most promising female talent and the National Radio Council Award's First Place Certificate of Merit. She was so popular that the Madame Alexander doll company made a doll modeled after her.

Alene read fairy tales to children on her radio and TV program. *Image by lukeruk on Shutterstock.*

In addition to telling stories, Alene also wrote them, publishing fifty books for young readers in her lifetime. Recognizing the special requirements for children's literature, she and Ross started their own children's book publishing company in 1962, Rolton House Publishers.

Her husband died in 1973, but even after his death, Alene stayed active in writing and performing. She became the president of the Pioneer Memorial Theater in Salt Lake City, serving until 1980. Alene died in Salt Lake City in 1986. Her headstone reads, "Alene Olsen Dalton Chapin. The Story Princess, Beloved by All." After her death, *My Picture Book of Song* went out of print. Erla Young, the only surviving collaborator, decided to reprint a fiftieth anniversary edition in 1997 for nostalgia's sake.

To her surprise, the book once again took off, selling thousands of copies.

Chapter 23

JUANITA BROOKS

Nothing but the Truth

It began with blood and a secret that would not stay silent. Nephi Johnson was an old, respected pioneer living in Mesquite, Nevada, in 1919. He had known Latter-day Saint church leader Joseph Smith and played an important role in establishing several southern Utah settlements. Juanita Leavitt, the granddaughter of his friend Dudley Leavitt, had a keen interest in history, and he had asked her to take some time with him to write down his life story—things he had seen but never spoken about. She agreed but put it off. Then, she got word that Nephi was dying.

Juanita felt guilty that she had delayed interviewing Nephi and hurried to his sickbed. There, she found a man delirious and apparently tortured. He prayed and preached in fevered confusion and cried out. His eyes opened wide, and he screamed, "Blood! Blood! Blood!"

Alarmed at Nephi's sufferings, Juanita asked his family what demons tormented him.

"He was at Mountain Meadows," they whispered to her.[73]

Juanita was struck and confused. The Mountain Meadows Massacre occurred during the Utah War in 1857, when the Baker-Fancher immigrant party headed for California was slaughtered while passing through Utah. About 120 men, women and children died in the attack, one of the darkest moments in Utah history. Juanita knew the traditional Utah story that it was mostly local Paiutes who had perpetrated the massacre. Latter-day Saint settler John D. Lee had been executed in 1877 for his involvement, but most of the Latter-day Saint population of Utah considered that the end of the tragedy. Outside of Utah and the "Mormon Corridor" of related colonies, everyone believed a different story: that Brigham Young had sent his band of mysterious, vigilante "Danites" to wipe out the immigrants.

Juanita had never given the massacre much thought. Her grandfather had been an associate of Nephi's at the time of the massacre, and after Nephi's death, the missed opportunity to hear his story and nagging questions about what really happened at Mountain Meadows haunted her.

Born in a Latter-day Saint colony in Nevada in 1888, Juanita had grown up with stories of her faith and its pioneers and developed a deep love of history. She had graduated from school and was working as a teacher in Nevada at the time of Nephi Johnson's death. Her curiosity about the massacre was piqued by his rantings, but the subject was taboo, and she was not ready to examine it yet.

That same year, in 1919, at age thirty-one, she married Ernest Pulsipher. They had one son together, but a little over a year after their marriage, Ernest died of cancer.

A young widow with an infant, Juanita made a decision. She moved to Provo, Utah, to go to college at Brigham Young University and study literature. With her degree, she returned to St. George, Utah, to teach English at Dixie College. She was also the dean of women at the school. She took a sabbatical from the college to earn her master's degree from

Juanita Brooks. *P018-061, WASH 018 Juanita Brooks Collection, Dixie State University Special Collections & Archives.*

Barnard College at Columbia University in New York.

When she returned to Utah in 1933, in the midst of the Great Depression, she found her program was being cut, so she resigned. She married a widower and sheriff named Will Brooks, who had four sons. Together, they had four more children. Mother to a mixed family of nine children, Juanita's life was extraordinarily busy. Yet she still loved history and writing, and she loved the truth.

During the Great Depression, the federal government sponsored the Works Progress Administration, which sought to employ artists and writers in works that would benefit the public. Juanita became involved with the WPA and with the Utah Historical Society collecting pioneer diaries. She wanted to preserve these stories, but she also wanted to understand more about the Mountain Meadows Massacre. She knew the stories being told by both sides were not the truth, and she would not feel easy until she knew what it was. Though the WPA ended when the United States entered World War II, Juanita continued her work with pioneer-era diaries as a field fellow for the Huntington Library, a major historical archive in California.

During the 1940s, Juanita also began writing a semi-autobiographical novel about life in the southern Mormon region of Nevada and Utah. But she set this aside because the Mountain Meadows Massacre still haunted her, and she wanted to focus on unraveling its secrets. She worked during the day taking care of her family, and at night she would research and write.

Most people in Utah accepted the official story of the massacre at face value, but there was an undercurrent of whispered stories and rumors about what really happened. The participants had taken the truth to their graves, and there was, perhaps, a fear that looking too closely would prove that Brigham Young had not been as innocent as the Latter-day Saint population would like to believe. Though church members do not consider their prophets infallible, they would certainly be shaken to think of them condoning murder. And while the Danites are only documented to have existed during the "Mormon War" in Missouri during the 1830s, non–Latter-day Saint visitors in Utah still feared they were roaming the territory to persecute them. These rumors played a large part in the ongoing dislike of Latter-day Saints and Utah by the general population. The Mountain Meadows Massacre was another factor driving anti-Mormon sentiments, and it appeared in many sensationalized accounts of the "Mormon problem."

Juanita was not going to write another sensational story about the massacre, nor was she going to ignore the facts that seemed obvious to her from her research. Some Latter-day Saint leaders discouraged her from publishing a book that might reflect badly on the church, since it was already viewed negatively by many in mainstream America. Juanita agonized over this concern. She knew she could even be excommunicated and lose her standing in the church and her community for what she wrote. Some local church members ostracized Juanita over her research, hurting her deeply. But she finally reached her conclusion: "Nothing but the truth can be good enough for the church to which I belong."[74]

In 1950, Stanford University Press published Juanita Brooks's *The Mountain Meadows Massacre*. In it, she concluded that it had been mainly the

Brigham Young led the Church of Jesus Christ of Latter-day Saints in Utah and left a controversial legacy. *Brady-Handy photograph collection, Library of Congress, Prints and Photographs Division.*

Mormon Militia of Cedar City that had perpetrated the massacre, with little involvement by the Paiutes. Brigham Young, she said, had not instigated or condoned the murders, but he had interfered with the investigations after the fact, allowing John D. Lee to be executed without pursuing others who participated in the massacre. This upset many church members, but Juanita was as even-handed as possible in describing the situation in Utah during the time. The U.S. government had sent Johnson's army to Utah to deal with the "Mormon problem," and having been driven from their homes and even murdered in the past, the Latter-day Saints were afraid. They reacted by lashing out at outsiders and using violent, divisive language in defending their rights—language that could easily lead to violent actions. Juanita did not use these circumstances as an excuse for the behavior of the militia members but helped the scholarly community understand the atmosphere in Utah during the Utah War. She also described the ongoing effects the aftermath of the massacre had on the church and its members.

The book was revolutionary. Juanita was not excommunicated, showing that Latter-day Saint historians did not have to fear the truths they might find in fair-minded research. It opened the way for other historians who were members of the Church of Jesus Christ of Latter-day Saints to move beyond faith-boosting narratives and tell a more complex story about the Mormon pioneers. Those in the next generation of Latter-day Saint historians, such as Leonard J. Arrington, were able to write "unsanitized" views of issues like polygamy thanks to the ground broken by Juanita. Laurel Thatcher Ulrich, Pulitzer Prize–winning Harvard historian and author and member of the Church of Jesus Christ of Latter-day Saints, recognized the example Juanita set for her, both as a woman trying to pursue an academic career and a family life and as a historian seeking to balance faith with facts.

Juanita continued to write about Utah and its history. She also campaigned for a proper monument to the victims of the Mountain Meadows Massacre. Families of the victims had placed memorials at the site beginning shortly after the massacre, but nothing official had been done to recognize them. Juanita died in 1989 after suffering from Alzheimer's, having never seen this ambition fulfilled. But in 1990, the State of Utah and the Church of Jesus Christ of Latter-day Saints lent their support to a more formal memorial installed by the descendants of the victims' families, and in 1999, the church worked with the victims' families to dedicate another memorial. In 2011, the church purchased an area believed to hold more victim grave sites in order to preserve the area.

Thanks to Juanita, much progress has been made in soothing the breaches caused by the massacre, the event itself is no longer a taboo subject and the Church of Jesus Christ of Latter-day Saints has become much more willing to open its history to public scrutiny.

Chapter 24

IVY BAKER PRIEST

Making Ends Meet

I vy Baker Priest never expected her autograph to be held by people all across the United States, but she knew that life could be unpredictable. She was known for saying, "The world is round, and the place which may seem like the end may also be only the beginning."[75]

Ivy's life demonstrated her philosophy well. She was born in 1905 in the booming gold mining town of Kimberly, Utah. The year 1905 was a peak one for Kimberly, with the Annie Laurie mine at full productivity and workers spending their time and money at the stores, dance hall, school and post office. The local stagecoach regularly shipped out stacks of gold bars worth $20,000 each. But within five years, the Annie Laurie was closed and Kimberly was a ghost town. Miners like Ivy's father, Orange Baker, moved on to other towns, chasing mining work.

The Baker family moved from place to place, barely scraping by, until Orange found work in the Bingham copper mine. Bingham was a more stable community than Kimberly, but mining is a dangerous job. When Ivy was seven, an accident disabled her father, leaving him unable to work.

The family was already living on the edge of poverty. Ivy's mother, Clara, took in boarders to help the family survive. The streets were just dirt, so in foul weather, the wet, tired miners who ate meals at the Baker home left a trail of mud, horse manure and other muck from the streets across the wooden floors. Sick of the mess, Clara began a campaign for the city to put in wooden sidewalks to make life cleaner and more pleasant for everyone. Her family physician, Dr. Fred E. Straup, was interested in her idea and

Streets of a Utah coal mining town in the 1930s. *Farm Security Administration–Office of War Information Photograph Collection, Library of Congress, Prints and Photographs Division.*

announced his plan to run for mayor and make the city more sanitary. Clara joined his campaign and helped gather support for him among the many immigrant residents of the town. Ivy went with her mother as they campaigned and helped the residents register to vote. During the election, Ivy babysat for people while they went to the polls. Ivy's interest in politics sprang from that election, which Dr. Straup won with the assistance of the Baker women.

As Ivy grew, so did her interest in politics. She held positions in Bingham High School's student leadership and graduated in 1924. She wanted to go to college to study law and pursue her interest in politics, but her family did not have the money to make that dream a reality. Instead, she worked selling movie tickets. She had a brief, unsuccessful marriage that took her to North Carolina. She returned to Utah in 1929 to work as a telephone operator and in a department store to support her mother and father. The Great Depression descended on the country, and everyone was struggling to make ends meet, but Ivy managed to take a few University of Utah extension courses. She also taught American history and citizenship classes to immigrants.

Despite her busy schedule, Ivy had not given up her interest in politics. She joined the Young Republicans, and in 1932, she served as a delegate to the GOP state convention. She ran for the Utah Congress in 1934, at age twenty-nine, but lost. As Ivy said, though, what might seem like an end could also be a beginning. In 1935, she married Roy Priest and moved to Bountiful, Utah. While raising their three children, Ivy continued her work with the Young Republicans, eventually becoming president. Of the challenge of balancing the different sides of her life, she said, "Any woman who has a career and a family automatically develops something in the way of two personalities, like two sides of a dollar bill, each different in design. But one can complement the other to make a valuable whole."[76]

But in 1939, tragedy struck. The Priests' young daughter Peggy died. Ivy was devastated. Her husband and her mother encouraged her to continue in the political involvement that she loved to assuage her grief. She threw herself back into her work and became Utah's Republican National committeewoman in 1944. She convinced Utah to pass a minimum wage law for working women, who were often paid less than men. In 1950, when she was forty-five, Ivy ran for the House of Representatives against incumbent Reva Bosone, who was the first Utah woman elected to the U.S. Congress. During the campaign, Ivy said, "I have been told that I haven't a ghost of a chance against Democratic incumbent Reva Beck Bosone. Be that as it may, I have had a chance to voice my concern over conditions as they exist under Representative Bosone."[77] The race made headlines for being the only one in the nation between two women, but Ivy lost.

After this defeat, Ivy turned her political focus in a different direction, becoming involved with Dwight D. Eisenhower's campaign for president. Ivy took the lead in encouraging women to vote. When Eisenhower won, with a large base of female supporters, he knew he owed some of his victory to Ivy's campaigning. He offered her a position in his administration: treasurer

Ivy Baker Priest as treasurer of the United States. *Used by permission, Utah State Historical Society.*

of the United States. She would be replacing Georgia Neese Clark, the first woman to hold the position.

Ivy was floored by the offer, but she accepted it. She practiced her signature over and over, knowing it would be used on all the dollar bills printed by the United States. When the first bills with her signature were printed, her hometown of Bountiful, Utah, ordered a huge number of them for local stores to distribute as change. Utah was excited to see the signature of one of its women on the dollar bill.

Ivy held the position of U.S. treasurer for eight years, from 1953 to 1961. She came to feel that growing up in poverty made her ideal for the position of treasurer. Though the U.S. treasurer does not sit on the president's cabinet, Ivy did have the opportunity to meet influential statesmen from around the country and the world, and she used her position to advance causes she was committed to, such as the Red Cross, the National Society for Crippled Children and Adults and the Utah and National Safety Councils. The woman who had not been able to afford college was awarded three honorary doctorates in recognition of her work.

In the midst of this exciting time for Ivy, in 1959, her husband, Roy, died. This was another painful blow for Ivy. When Eisenhower left office in 1961, she decided to move to California to be near her daughters. One, Pat Priest, was pursuing an acting career and would play Marilyn Munster on the sitcom *The Munsters*. In California, Ivy married again to Sidney Williams Stevens.

In 1966, Ivy decided to run for state treasurer of California, promising to invest California's revenues in a way that would yield higher returns. She won that campaign, being the first woman to be elected to a statewide office in California. She served alongside Ronald Reagan while he was governor, holding the position from 1967 until 1974 and working to fulfill her campaign promise. During the same period, she also became the chairwoman of the Easter Seals, an organization that raises money for people with disabilities.

In 1971, Ivy's son Roy died in a boating accident, and the next year, her third husband died. Ivy's health began to decline, and she was diagnosed with cancer. She decided her political career was finally at an end and she would spend her remaining time with the family she had left. She died in 1975 at age sixty-nine. The Women's Newspaper Editors and Publishers Association named her one of the twenty outstanding women of the twentieth century.

Chapter 25

MARY LUCILLE PERKINS BANKHEAD

A New Genesis

Mary Lucille Perkins Bankhead arrived early to the Daughters of Utah Pioneers meeting in Salt Lake City. She was the secretary of the organization and had been invited to speak to the group that day. But when she walked up to the front, the doorman shook his head and refused to open it.

In the 1930s, African Americans were not welcome at the front door of Utah establishments. The doorman expected Lucille to go around to the kitchen with the "help." Even famous African American performers like singer Ella Fitzgerald were not allowed in the front—sometimes they were not allowed into Utah hotels or restaurants at all unless they were performing there. There usually were no "No Blacks Allowed" signs in Utah, with its small black population, yet the unspoken rule still existed. But Lucille was a member of the Daughters of Utah Pioneers just like the other women who had walked through the front door, and she stood her ground. One of her philosophies in life was "If I want to go someplace, I go."[78] Finally, the doorman relented and let her in. On account of her quiet stubbornness, many doors would open in her lifetime.

Lucille had a pioneer ancestry that was hard to rival, even in Utah. She was a descendant of Green Flake, the slave who reputedly drove Brigham Young into the Salt Lake Valley in 1847. She was also related by marriage to Jane Manning James, the free black pioneer who was friends with church founder Joseph Smith and his wife, Emma, and was unofficially adopted into their family. Even though Lucille was born in

Segregation was common throughout the United States in the 1930s and '40s. *Library of Congress, Prints and Photographs Division.*

1902, long after the last handcarts and wagons had arrived in Utah, she had her own pioneering to do.

Her family had a homestead just outside Salt Lake City where they grew peaches and black currants. Since both of her parents were busy all day with farm work, Lucille ended up doing most of the cooking for the family, which she enjoyed. Hard work was an accepted fact of life for Lucille, and she lived and farmed on her family's homestead all her life, until old age forced her to quit. The Perkins children also had time for fun and learning, making frequent visits to the library. Their mother often read to them from the Bible and Book of Mormon, and the children taught their father to read. Growing up, Lucille's neighbors were generally friendly, and she did not experience much racial tension with them. They accepted her for who she was, and she did not see why everyone could not do the same. She said, "I cannot understand why some people…have to be racist.…My blood is just as red as theirs even if my skin is dark. The Lord made us all."[79]

In 1922, Lucille married Thomas Bankhead, also a descendent of slaves brought to Utah by early pioneers. Though Thomas would attend social functions at the church, the treatment he and their sons received from members made them uninterested in being part of worship services. He would sit out in the car and wait for Lucille and their children to finish their worship services, even in the bitter cold winter weather. Their sons enjoyed the church activities when they were young, but as they grew up, they began to feel alienated. Until 1978, African American men could not join the priesthood of the Church of Jesus Christ of Latter-day Saints, which was otherwise open to all male members. This led the Bankhead boys to become disillusioned and stay away from church meetings.

Despite the difficulties, Lucille remained an active member of the church. She had come to believe the teachings of the church at a young age, and nothing would deter her from that. She said, "It does not matter to me what the other man does or what he feels. I do not have to answer for nobody but Lucille. I try to live right. I try to be kind to all." On her eighth birthday—the youngest age at which she could officially join the Church of Jesus Christ of Latter-day Saints—she had decided it was time to be baptized. She announced this to a neighbor who was also a church elder, and he baptized her right then in an irrigation ditch.

The restrictions on blacks holding the priesthood were still painful to her. She felt they came from man and not God and prayed that they would change. She often told others that she felt God had told her that the change was coming.

Lucille also associated with non–Latter-day Saint members of Salt Lake City's black community. She was friends with some of the black members of the Baptist church, and though they sometimes clashed over religion, she took part in their activities. One of the Salt Lake City clubs she joined was an African American arts and crafts club. In 1939, a Salt Lake City realtor drafted a petition to force all of the city's African Americans into a single ghetto. It was a common practice in the United States at the time to either officially or unofficially segregate property so that African Americans and other people of color could not own, rent or buy real estate in the more desirable parts of cities

Lucille Perkins Bankhead (*right*) with her mother, Martha J. Perkins Howell. *Used by permission, Utah State Historical Society.*

and towns. Over one thousand people signed the Salt Lake City petition and took it to the state senate, which considered turning it into law.

Lucille's arts and crafts club, along with other African American organizations, heard of the proposed law and headed to the state capitol to stage a sit-in. Lucille had an infant with her, but she took the baby along. Just as with the doorman at the Daughters of Utah Pioneers meeting, she was willing to stay as long as it took. The peaceful protest drew attention, and many of the state lawmakers decided they would not support the racist proposition, defeating the proposed law. This did not stop the practice entirely, however, as some people would add clauses to real estate contracts saying that the property could only be sold to Caucasians.

The changes to racist policies in Utah were slow, but they did come. In 1948, the Supreme Court ruled race clauses in real estate contracts unconstitutional. About the same time, the white owner of the popular Lagoon resort, Robert Freed, desegregated the resort's dance hall and swimming pool, opening the way for further desegregation in Utah. By the end of the 1950s, African American entertainers—and Lucille Bankhead—could walk in the front door and use the same hotels and restaurants as everyone else.

Despite the priesthood restrictions, there was still a small but vibrant African American Latter-day Saint population in Utah, both those like Lucille with long pioneer heritages and new converts. Recognizing the difficulties and prejudices faced by black church members, in 1971, church leaders started a program known as the Genesis Group to offer them support. Lucille was one of the founding members of this group, and church leadership appointed her to be the group's first Relief Society president.

Lucille recalled many tearful nights as she struggled with the challenges she and her fellow African American Latter-day Saints encountered on a daily basis. They were sometimes ridiculed by African Americans of other faiths, faced discrimination by white Latter-day Saints and often saw families divided over the issue of church membership. Lucille was responsible for helping them deal with these and other trials and heartaches.

In 1978, the members of the Genesis Group and other black Latter-day Saints finally received every benefit available to other church members. When Lucille first got the call about it, she thought someone was teasing her. Only when she got a second call did she believe that her years of faithful devotion had finally paid off. It was one of the most wonderful things she had ever heard. Male African Americans could now hold the priesthood, and females like Lucille could participate in ceremonies in the temple, which included being sealed to family members forever.

The Genesis Group disbanded for a while after 1978 but was reinstated when church leadership recognized that African American church members still faced unique challenges. Lucille also saw that they still had a long way to go. She continued to serve in the church and outside of it. She volunteered cooking at a nursing home for black patients, and when she found that some of the nurses were neglecting the elderly patients, she protested to the management until all the patients were getting the proper care.[80]

Lucille's persistent faith and determination made her a backbone among the African American Latter-day Saints and the rest of Utah's black population. In 1987, she was the inaugural speaker at Utah's Ebony Rose Black History Conference. When she passed away in Salt Lake City in 1994, she had lived through almost the entire twentieth century and seen African Americans gain many rights in Utah and move much closer to being treated equally by the rest of Utah society.

Chapter 26

KATE B. CARTER AND HELEN Z. PAPANIKOLAS

Saving History

The 1960s and '70s were a time of cultural revolution in the United States. Feminism and the civil rights movement slowly changed the way women and minorities were treated in society. The revolution affected the study of history as well. Prior to the 1960s, most history was political and economic, focused mainly on upper-class white men. Though politics, economics and the accomplishments of notable white males are important for understanding the past, the focus on them left an incomplete picture, with very little information about the experiences and contributions of women, children, people of color and the poor—those who rarely left written records or great monuments. Local and family histories were looked down on as the work of amateurs.

Thanks in part to the efforts of two Utah women, the Beehive State was well ahead of the curve when it came to recording and studying the lives of the "common" people. Kate Bearnson Carter and Helen Zeese Papanikolas led the effort to save the stories of everyday men and women from Utah's history.

Catherine Vigdis Bearnson, who went by Kate, was born in Spanish Fork, Utah, in 1891 to immigrant parents from Iceland and Denmark. Her father had a great love of history, which he passed on to his daughter. Both of her parents stressed the importance of education and filled their home with as many books as they could afford. Kate later said, "I have never yet seen a great reader who was unhappy," and when asked what she would do differently if she could live her life again, she decided she would spend less money on food and more on books.[81]

Kate B. Carter
(*center*) with a
historical cart.
*Used by permission,
Utah State
Historical Society.*

One of her neighbors growing up was an elderly man who could not write in English, so he asked Kate to record his life story for him when she was twelve, beginning a lifelong dedication to preserving the oral histories of Utah pioneers.

Kate graduated from Stevens-Henager Business College in Salt Lake City and continued her studies by taking classes at Brigham Young University and the University of Utah. In 1914, she married Austin Carter. Her interest in pioneer history led her to join the Daughters of Utah Pioneers, but she was disappointed to find that it was more of a social club than a historical organization. She felt that people could not understand the present without knowing the past, and she developed a passion for researching Utah's early pioneers. She was most interested in the "ordinary" immigrants who came to Utah and what their lives were like.

By the 1930s, the first pioneer generation was rapidly dying off, and Kate understood that if their stories were not saved, they would be lost forever. She set to work collecting and publishing these stories. Some of her works were *Our Pioneer Heritage*, *Heart Throbs of the West* and *Treasures of Pioneer History*, as well as biographies of important pioneer women such as poet Eliza R. Snow and Louisa Barnes Pratt, the first female missionary for the Church of Jesus Christ of Latter-day Saints. She also encouraged people to record their own stories for future generations. Austin and their three children all helped her with her work.

Though the Daughters of Utah Pioneers had sometimes hesitated to recognize the contributions of African Americans to the settlement of Utah, Kate sought out their stories as well, collecting oral histories of some of Utah's early black pioneers, including those who had come to the territory as slaves. She published these in *The Story of the Negro Pioneer* in 1965.

Katie served as president of the Daughters of Utah Pioneers from 1941 to 1976, when her declining health finally caught up with her and she passed away. During her presidency, she transformed the group into the more serious historical organization that she had envisioned when she joined. She used the proceeds from her books and contributions collected over a period of fourteen years to found the Daughters of Utah Pioneers Museum in Salt Lake City, preserving stories and artifacts from pioneer Utah. She had been involved in the Days of '47 Parade and worked to place hundreds of historical markers throughout Utah to teach people about local historical events.

For her efforts to preserve history, she was added to the Utah Women's Hall of Fame and awarded the Order of the Falcon from Iceland, her father's native country and a nation very interested in history and literature. The American Association for State and Local History gave her a distinguished service award for her historical work.

Kate's work was an important first step in preserving Utah's history, and it would be followed up by Helen Z. Papanikolas. The daughter of Greek immigrants, Helen Zeese was born in a mining town near Castle Gate, Utah, in 1917. She grew up in Helper, Utah, surrounded by her Greek community but also with the diversity and tumult of a Utah mining town: strikes, mine explosions and ethnic tensions. She hid her Greek books from fellow students so they would not tease her about them and witnessed the KKK burning a cross in the railroad yard. She remembered "the monstrous thing called recess where Americans and Mormons stood on one side of no man's land and immigrant children on the other, shouting and daring each

Helen Zeese Papanikolas. *Used by permission, Utah State Historical Society.*

other to cross over."[82] Helen's father brought adult cousins in to help protect his children from anti-immigrant violence, and in 1933, he moved the family to Salt Lake City, where Helen finished school.

After high school, Helen attended the University of Utah and served as editor of the *Pen* literary magazine until she graduated in 1939. She planned to be a doctor, but her professors recognized her talent for writing and storytelling and encouraged her to pursue a literary career instead. She began writing, and she married Nick Papanikolas in 1941. While raising their two children, she continued her literary pursuits, crafting stories influenced by her Greek upbringing.

In 1950, the *Utah Historical Quarterly* approached Helen and asked her to write something about Utah's Greek community. Previously, like most 1950s historical journals, the *UHQ* had focused on Anglo history. Helen's 1954 article "The Greeks of Carbon County" began to change the way Utah history was studied and documented, opening the way for more ethnic studies and putting Utah a decade ahead of historical trends in the rest of the country.

Helen had a skill and passion for oral history, and she continued collecting the stories of people who had often been overlooked in Utah history: African Americans, Japanese who had stayed in Utah after the prison camps of World War II, Jews, Hispanics, Italians, Chinese, eastern Europeans and others. In 1976, the state asked her to create a book incorporating her research, *The Peoples of Utah*, as part of the celebration of the two-hundred-year anniversary of the American Revolution. This led her to found the Peoples of Utah Institute to continue and broaden her work, as well as the Hellenic Cultural Museum in Salt Lake to celebrate the contributions of Greek Americans to Utah's history.

She continued her writing as well, publishing works of nonfiction and fiction about the Greek experience in the American West, including *Toil and Rage in a New Land*, *An Amulet of Greek Earth* and *Rain in the Valley*. University presses published her works, giving ethnic history and folklore respectability and encouraging others to study them as well. These works led Helen to be considered one of the preeminent ethnic historians in the United States and earned her invitations to speak around the world. She and her husband established scholarships for ethnic minorities studying in Utah, and she mentored many young historians. She served on the boards for the *Utah Historical Quarterly* and Utah Endowment for the Humanities and encouraged minority groups in Utah to tell their stories. Her work helped to expand the understanding of Utah's history and of what it meant to be a Utahn.

Helen received numerous awards for her work, showing the many communities she affected, such as the Japanese American Citizens League Award and the Brotherhood Award of the National Conference of Christians and Jews, and the University of Utah awarded her an honorary doctorate degree.

By the time of her death in 2004, the entire landscape of history in Utah and the United States had changed dramatically, with social and cultural history becoming more popular in colleges than political history. Thanks to the work of Kate B. Carter and Helen Papanikolas, Utah's history was well preserved, and the study of ordinary people and ordinary lives was widely accepted as important to understanding the whole spectrum of the human story.

Chapter 27

CHIEKO NISHIMURA OKAZAKI

Teaching Hope

Chieko Nishimura Okazaki was excited to move to Utah from Hawaii after World War II and become a teacher there. During World War II, anti-Japanese sentiment in Utah ran high, as many people lost family members in the war against Japan, and Japanese Americans were imprisoned in camps in Utah and elsewhere. But Chieko hoped she could move past that. Raised a Buddhist, she had joined the Church of Jesus Christ of Latter-day Saints in Hawaii and looked forward to coming to the place she thought of as "Zion"—where people lived together in unity and happiness. Before Pearl Harbor, the various races and ethnic groups of Hawaii had coexisted in relative harmony, and Chieko hoped to find a similar situation in a state where many people shared her adopted faith.

Her husband, Edward Okazaki, a fellow Japanese Hawaiian, had served with the 442nd Regimental Combat Unit, an all–Japanese American combat group in World War II that became the most decorated military unit in American history. He and the other Japanese Americans had worked hard and sacrificed to prove their loyalty to the United States. Now, he wanted to get his graduate degree in social work at the University of Utah.

Chieko got a job teaching second grade in Salt Lake City and prepared to meet her new pupils. As soon as word reached the parents that their children were going to be taught by a Japanese American woman, though, three of them pulled their children from her class. Many of the others were wary. Chieko was hurt, but she understood that they were afraid. Many of their families had lost fathers, husbands, sons or brothers fighting Japan in the Pacific during the war.

The 442nd Regimental Combat Team, an all–Japanese American unit in World War II, was one of the most decorated units in U.S. military history. *Bureau of Public Relations, U.S. War Department, Library of Congress, Prints and Photographs Division.*

Her family had been afraid, too, in Hawaii when Pearl Harbor was bombed—both of the imperial Japanese troops and of how people would react to them because of their Japanese ancestry. Chieko and her mother gathered every Japanese item they owned and burned them, watching the memories of their past crumble to ash. But Chieko looked at herself in the mirror and realized she could do nothing about her Japanese features. She contemplated what her identity meant: she had a Japanese face, but she had never been to Japan. Hawaii was her home, and she was an American. She shared her neighbors' fears of Japanese planes and submarines and thought about how she would run away from the Japanese. But she could not run away from herself. She had to accept her identity with all of its complexities.[83]

So, despite the reaction of her students' parents in Utah, Chieko was determined to win over the children in her class. Her principal in Utah was very supportive and encouraged her to move forward. Chieko showed up on the first day of school with a brightly colored dress and a flower tucked behind her ear. She had something positive to say to each student as they entered the school. The children loved her, and the three children moved from her class begged to be allowed back in. The principal told their parents that they had missed their chance.

Even at church, people acted uncertain or afraid of the Okazakis. The white church members wondered if these people with Japanese features could really be Latter-day Saints. Chieko and Edward addressed this by being friendly and outgoing to show others that they were not enemies. They won over most of their fellow church members, and Chieko did not let the others affect her positive attitude or her efforts to be a compassionate Christian. She remembered the teaching that her Buddhist mother had passed on to her that if she knew the truth—about herself or her beliefs—it did not matter if others did not. She said, "We just held on and tried to look at the doctrines of the gospel rather than how people behaved sometimes, and believed that our Father in Heaven and Jesus Christ would not look at us as any different from white members."[84]

Despite sometimes facing prejudice, Chieko continued to be actively involved in the Church of Jesus Christ of Latter-day Saints. Her husband finished his education and eventually got a job in Colorado. Chieko enjoyed the greater diversity there, especially among members of the Church of Jesus Christ of Latter-day Saints. In 1961, she was asked to join the board of the church's Young Women's program, becoming the first person of color to serve on a general board (one of the organizations that oversees activities in the entire church).

In 1968, church leaders asked Edward to establish the church's Japan Okinawa mission, which meant moving to Japan. Chieko oversaw the children's Primary program, the Young Women's program and the adult women's Relief Society activities in Japan. She also organized the Mormon Pavilion at the Expo '70 world fair in Osaka, Japan.

When the couple returned to the United States, Chieko decided to get her master's degree in education. She continued to teach, eventually becoming a school principal, where she made the effort to know each of the five hundred students in her school.

She also continued to be active in the leadership of the Church of Jesus Christ of Latter-day Saints. She served on the general boards for the Primary and the Relief Society organizations. In 1990, she was called to be first counselor in the Relief Society general presidency—again making history as the first non-Caucasian women to serve in the presidency of a Latter-day Saint general presidency. She was also unusual among Utah Latter-day

Chieko Okazaki with her students. *Used by permission, Utah State Historical Society.*

Saints at the time because she was a working woman and had only two children. In 1992, Edward died, leaving her a widow.

Luckily, she was not afraid to stand out. The Church of Jesus Christ of Latter-day Saints was becoming a more international organization, and she knew firsthand the struggle that some encountered feeling welcome in a church that, on the surface, was based around large Caucasian families.

Even those who seemed to be typical Latter-day Saint women often felt that there was not a place for them in the organization or that they did not matter. Chieko wanted everyone to know that they mattered and that strength came to individuals and organizations by embracing differences. She made an effort when traveling around the world to be able to deliver talks in the native languages of the people she was speaking too. She also was the first general church leader to broach such topics as sexual abuse, drug addiction, infertility, blended families, homosexuality and racism over the pulpit. Many people were shocked to hear previously taboo topics brought into the open, but it proved to be healing, as those who had struggled in silence now felt they were not alone and could talk about their own experiences.

Chieko's mixture of honesty about hard topics and hopeful faith made her a popular speaker and writer, authoring a number of best-selling books. Recordings of her talks were also bestsellers, and people packed into auditoriums to hear her speak. She served on the board of trustees for Southern Virginia University and the Children's Reading Foundation of Utah, and she established a scholarship for social work students at the University of Utah in memory of her husband. After she survived breast cancer, she spoke openly about the experience and what she learned from it. When failing health forced her to move into an assisted living facility, she said she was grateful for the chance to make friends with the other residents.[85]

At Chieko's death in 2011, she was widely mourned by Latter-day Saints and others touched by her writing and speaking. The woman who had come to Utah to teach had the opportunity to educate far more people and influence more lives than she ever expected.

Chapter 28

EMMA LOU THAYNE

Poet of Peace

Where can I turn for peace?

This line, penned by poet Emma Lou Thayne, reflected a question that was a refrain in her life. In 1971, at age forty-seven, she was on the Young Women's General Board of the Church of Jesus Christ of Latter-day Saints. She had four children at home and needed a back surgery that would force her to quit teaching at the University of Utah midway through the term. Worse, one of her daughters, Becky, struggled with bipolar disorder and both anorexia and bulimia. She and her family were hurting, struggling, reaching out for comfort and reassurance that all would be well again.

In the midst of this painful time, the Young Women's General Board asked Emma Lou and composer Joleen G. Meredith to write a song for a special conference for young women. Joleen was also suffering with mental illness at the time. Weighed down by her trials and the anguish she saw in the lives around her, Emma Lou put her pain into words, writing lyrics that began, "Where can I turn for peace? Where is my solace?"

She shared the lyrics with Joleen over the phone, and the composer began playing a tune on the piano. Together, they created the song "Where Can I Turn for Peace," which they called a "mental illness hymn." The answer that both of these women found for their personal struggles was in their faith in God, that he was there, reaching out to them in their times of suffering.[86]

But Emma Lou's faith was not a passive thing, and neither were her responses to difficulties. An active tennis champion and writer, she had a drive to *do*. She and her daughter Becky decided to co-author a book about

Becky's three-year struggle with mental illnesses. *Hope and Recovery* was praised as an honest, inspiring account of their family's experience. They went a step further and used the proceeds to set up a scholarship at the University of Utah for students studying mental illnesses. This was one of many examples of how Emma Lou tackled the challenges she saw around her and found beauty and meaning in life's experiences.

Emma Lou Warner was born in Salt Lake City in 1924. She grew up with three brothers and was inspired by the natural wonders she saw around her in the Utah landscape. She studied at the University of Utah during World War II, and when it was over, the demand for professors was so

Emma Lou Thayne. *Special Collections, J. Willard Marriott Library, the University of Utah.*

high that she was able to continue at the university as an English teacher. In 1950, she married Melvin Thayne. They lived in California while he went to school at Stanford University and then moved back to Utah to raise their five daughters. Emma wrote and published poetry and prose and, in 1968, earned her master's degree in creative writing at the University of Utah. She continued teaching English at the university and also established and coached the women's tennis team there, using her own money to pay for the gas to attend distant meets since the university did not fund women's sports.[87]

Outside of her work at the university, she served on the board of the Utah Arts Council and Odyssey House and was the only woman on the board for the *Deseret News*. She always advocated for truth and accuracy in writing and in journalism.

That desire for truth and accuracy permeated her own works as well. She published fourteen volumes of poetry and prose, exploring real issues, questions and inspiration she had as a woman, a mother and a member of the Church of Jesus Christ of Latter-day Saints. She and Pulitzer Prize–winning Latter-day Saint author and historian Laurel Thatcher Ulrich worked together on *All God's Critters Got a Place in the Choir*, a collection of poems, essays and letters where the two women explore what it means to be so many things: feminists, environmentalists, mothers, wives, educators and women of faith. They reflected the concerns, struggles, hopes and triumphs many women feel trying to balance their diverse roles in a beautiful but imperfect world.

Emma Lou had a strong sense of the kinship of all people and used her writing to campaign for peace among the nations. She was involved in AIDS awareness campaigns, women's rights and educational exchanges with the Soviet Union in hopes of bringing peace to individuals and nations. She was also concerned about damage to the natural environment and wrote about the need to protect that beauty, such as in her poetry collection *How Much for the Earth?*

Utah's environment had been directly affected by the nuclear age, as uranium mining poisoned the Navajo Nation and the federal government tested nuclear bombs in the neighboring Nevada desert, knowing that the fallout would drift into the "empty" region of southern Utah. The affected "Downwinders" in southern Utah suffered increased cancer rates, sterility and birth defects, while the government denied any culpability for decades. Emma Lou and other Utah authors like Terry Tempest Williams used their writing to plead with the governments and peoples of the world to avoid further harm from the irresponsible use of nuclear power.

Nuclear testing in Nevada in the 1950s did not give consideration to the people exposed to the resulting radioactive fallout. *Library of Congress, Prints and Photographs Division.*

In 1986, when Emma was sixty-two, a metal bar flew through the windshield of the car she was riding in, striking her in the face. The bar broke her jaw, damaged her eye and left her with multiple facial fractures. She underwent surgeries and a long recovery time, spending seven months unable to lift her head. After the accident, the woman who had always been known for her active life and positive attitude struggled with her physical and mental health. As with other dark times in her life, she turned the experience into one of spiritual examination. Out of this struggle came her last book, *The Place of Knowing*. In it, she explored the journey of recovery and the wonders of everyday life. She summed up what she felt was her purpose in life, saying, "I could try, in telling my stories, to make the light…real and moving.…Out of the grace offered to me, I could ask for ways to offer it to others."[88]

After her recovery, she could no longer play singles tennis or be as active as she once was, but she continued to work for peace and treat everyone she met as a friend. She volunteered at a senior center, helping the residents tell their life stories. Her last position in her local church congregation was as a greeter, where she would hug everyone who came into the chapel. She was awarded several honorary doctorate degrees for her work, as well as the David O. McKay Humanities Award and the Gandhi Award for Peace.

Emma died of congestive heart failure in 2014 at ninety years old. She was positive to the end, grateful that the heart failure would not cause her to suffer for long. Over one thousand people attended her funeral, remembering her sense of humor and love of everyone. The funeral closed with a rendition of her hymn, "Where Can I Turn for Peace," a reminder of her tireless life's work to bring peace to others.

Chapter 29

BARBARA GREENLEE TOOMER

A World without Barriers

Barbara Greenlee Toomer was not afraid to speak up when she thought something was not right. As a college student in California, she was outraged when one of her professors was removed from his teaching job because he would not sign an anti-communist document that he thought was wrong. Though communist Russia and China represented real threats to the United States, some people like U.S. senator Joseph McCarthy capitalized on this fear to strengthen their own political positions, often stripping people of their positions and livelihoods without proof. Barbara felt her professor was one of those and said, "Basically, at that point, I decided there's something wrong somewhere, that there was discrimination going on."[89]

No one listened to Barbara's outrage over her professor, but later in life, her willingness to raise her voice in protest would change Utah and the United States.

Born in 1929, Barbara grew up in California during the Great Depression. She remembered living in the back of her father's office as he struggled to find work. As a girl, she found enjoyment in arts and sewing and thrived in Girl Scouts and sports, especially swimming, where she won several medals. She graduated from high school in 1947, and with both of her parents able to work again in the booming postwar economy, she started college. She wanted to study at UCLA but could not afford to finish there, so she attended St. Joseph's College of Nursing, graduating in 1952.

Barbara enjoyed work as a nurse, especially the excitement of the surgery unit and labor and delivery, but the job was not perfect. She had one male nursing colleague, and she discovered that he was earning more than she was for the same work. She spoke up about the disparity, but her supervisors informed her that it was fair for him to earn more because, as a man, he would have to support a family and she would not. Once again, she knew it was not right, but no one was willing to listen.

Dissatisfied, Barbara looked for other opportunities. Her sister had joined the U.S. Air Force as part of the efforts of the Korean War to stop the spread of communism in Asia. Barbara decided to join the United States Army Nurse Corps, enlisting as a first lieutenant. While she was serving in 1953 in Fort Bragg, North Carolina, she married Captain Gerald Ross Toomer.

In 1956, Barbara had her first child. The doctors offered the child something revolutionary: a vaccination for polio. Polio was always present, one of the nightmares of parents. The disease was not treatable and could result in paralysis, a lifetime in an iron lung or death. Barbara remembered that her father had been disdainful of President Franklin D. Roosevelt, who was in a wheelchair because of polio. Her father, like many others, felt that those with disabilities were somehow shameful and had no real place in society. Barbara not only agreed to the vaccine for her child but also wanted one for herself. At the time, however, the vaccine was available in limited quantities, so they only offered it to the most vulnerable populations. Her child got the vaccine, but Barbara did not.

Not long after, Barbara experienced excruciating headaches and back pain. Her husband called in a doctor, who returned the verdict: polio. An epidemic of it swept through the army base where they were living, putting several people, including Barbara, in the hospital. While she suffered through a feverish delirium, her husband looked desperately for someone to help care for their child, but everyone was afraid of catching the disease, not sure if the vaccine would be enough to keep the child from getting ill. Even Barbara's mother refused to help care for her grandchild. Finally, one of the Toomers' neighbors, a pipe-smoking woman with a heavy Tennessee accent whom she and her husband had looked down on, agreed to help care for their child. Barbara said after that she would never say anything bad about anyone again.[90]

Barbara's child never became sick with polio, thanks to the vaccine, but Barbara was paralyzed from the neck down. She was in the hospital for months, working with physical therapists to try to regain some movement in her legs and arms. Her father, who had so despised President Roosevelt's disability, refused to visit her, and some of her friends turned their backs on her as well, forcing her to recognize that she would no longer be welcome everywhere by everyone. She later said, "That feeling still exists, that disability is the most awful thing that could possibly happen to a person."[91]

When she did return home, she had regained some use of her hands, but even the smallest tasks were difficult for her. She would cry and beg her husband to help, but he would sit next to her and say gently, "If I do it for you you're never going to do it for yourself."[92]

Barbara was angry, but she knew he was right. She directed her anger into her recovery. She did not view her disability as unfair; it was just something that had happened. As she learned to be independent with her wheelchair, she developed the philosophy that she did not want to just live with her disability; she wanted to be a disabled person who fully lived.

Ross worked with computers and electronics and helped her invent devices allowing her to be as independent as possible. He retired from the army, and they moved to Idaho to be near his parents. Utah's economy was booming thanks to the many military institutions in the state, and Ross found work there, moving the family to Salt Lake City. Barbara decided not to let her disability stop her from living. She was involved in the Civil Air Patrol and served as a delegate for the Democratic Party and a Latter-day Saint Relief Society president.

Barbara's disability made her more aware of the difficulties that other people with physical differences suffered, whether they were in a wheelchair, blind, deaf or otherwise disabled. She became active in helping people who were disabled to live their lives to the fullest and in helping able-bodied people understand the difficulties she and others faced every day. She did not just want to see disabled people doing as they were expected to do; she wanted them to be able to live the life they actually wanted. In 1981, she founded the Utah Independent Living Center and helped to start Advocates for Utah Handicapped.

Over the next couple of years, she thought about how difficult it was for people with disabilities to get around. Many buses and other public transportation in Utah were not designed to fit wheelchairs or be accessible to people who had difficulty walking. Federal law required cities to update their buses, but many transportation authorities fought to have the law delayed or overturned. Barbara tried speaking about the problem and writing letters, but as with so many other times in her life, no one seemed interested in listening.

Inspired by nonviolent protesters like Martin Luther King Jr. and Rosa Parks, she organized "crawl-ons," where disabled people would use the buses by crawling or pulling themselves up the stairs and dragging their wheelchairs

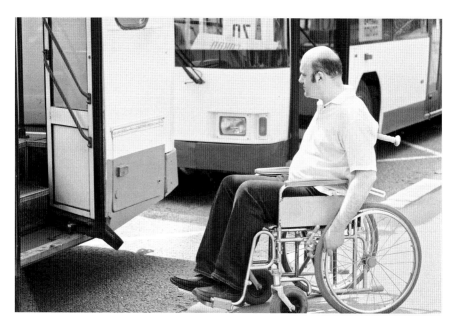

Barbara Toomer's efforts helped people understand the importance of accessible public transportation. *Image by gillmar on Shutterstock.*

after them to demonstrate the need for buses with ramps. When that did not spur changes, she and other disability rights advocates chained themselves to the inaccessible buses. Barbara and the other protesters were arrested. In fact, Barbara was arrested thirty-five times in protests across the country, but she did not quit until the transportation authorities provided buses that everyone could use, regardless of their ability to walk or climb stairs.

Barbara continued working for disability rights in the 1990s, protesting fare hikes for disabled persons and cab companies that were not wheelchair-friendly. She represented Utah in the Washington, D.C. protests that led to the passage of the Americans with Disabilities Act, which required public places to be accessible to all Americans, whether or not they needed a wheelchair or other assistive devices to navigate their environment. She was involved in organizing the Disabled Rights Action Committee to speak up for people with disabilities in the public arena.

Her work on behalf of people with disabilities was recognized with several awards, including the Martin Luther King Jr. Drum Major Award, the Rosa Parks Award from the Salt Lake NAACP and the National Organization for Women's Woman of Courageous Action Lifetime Achievement Award. All this time she remained active with her children and grandchildren. She cared for her husband after he had several heart attacks, and when her mother developed dementia, Barbara took her into her home, caring for her as well.

Barbara continued her campaign for equal access, especially with a focus on allowing people with disabilities to live in their homes rather than have to go to institutions (she advised Presidents Bill Clinton and George W. Bush on this issue), until her death in 2018 at eighty-eight years old. She donated her body to the University of Utah School of Medicine, a last act in service to greater understanding of disabilities. Though she could not erase every unfairness from the world, by constantly raising her voice, she made herself heard and broke down many walls holding back people of all abilities.

NOTES

Chapter 1

1. Iverson, "Chipeta."
2. Lyman-Whitney, "Chipeta."

Chapter 2

3. Wells, Diaries, 1844–1920.
4. Ibid.
5. Mason, "Emmeline B. Wells."
6. Wells, Diaries, 1844–1920, 89.

Chapter 3

7. Lythgoe, "Negro Slavery in Utah," 27–28.
8. Williams, "Remembering Utah's Forgotten Black Pioneers."
9. Coleman, "Blacks in Utah."

Chapter 4

10. Helm, "Reminiscence."
11. Snodgrass, *Frontier Women and Their Art*, 261.
12. Reeder and Holbrook, "Thirteenth Ward Relief Society Covenant."
13. Cooper-Rompato, "Women Inventors in Utah Territory."
14. "Some Startling Charges," *Salt Lake Tribune*.

Chapter 6

15. Hanson, "Down to Vicksburg," 286–309.
16. Worster, *A River Running West*, 216.
17. Northrup, *World's Fair*, 173.
18. Worster, *A River Running West*, 536.
19. Ibid., 570.

Chapter 7

20. Fields, "How a Mormon Pioneer Woman."
21. Lieber and Sillito, *Letters from Exile*, 210.
22. Ibid., 225.
23. "Martha Hughes Cannon."
24. Graña, *Pioneer, Polygamist, Politician*.

Chapter 8

25. Reeve, "Just Who Was the Outlaw Queen Etta Place?"
26. Brulliard, "Wild West Josie."

Chapter 9

27. "Miss Claire Ferguson," *Salt Lake Tribune*.
28. "She Has Power to Arrest," *Salt Lake Tribune*.
29. "Nurse Goes Free," *Salt Lake Tribune*.

30. "She Has Power to Arrest," *Salt Lake Tribune*.
31. Dobner, "She Was a Teen Mother."

Chapter 10

32. Papanikolas, "Exiled Greeks."

Chapter 11

33. Babcock, "Pantomime," 223–24.
34. Ibid.
35. Ibid.
36. Tanner, "Shakespeare Among the Saints," 82–115.
37. Ratliffe, "Maud May Babcock," 56–62.
38. Babcock, "Pantomime," 223.

Chapter 12

39. Jones, "Sun Dance."
40. "Zitkála-Šá."

Chapter 13

41. Barkhorn, "'Vote No on Women's Suffrage.'"

Chapter 14

42. Clark, "Aviation Pioneer."
43. "Stricken Aviators Rushed to Hospital," *Salt Lake Tribune*.
44. "Wounded Americans Superb Maintain Spirit," *Salt Lake Tribune*.
45. Topping, "Utah Catholic Woman in World War I."

Chapter 15

46. Rivera de Martinez, Oral History, 16.
47. Skinner, "Honoring a Heritage."
48. Rivera de Martinez, Oral History, 15.

Chapter 16

49. Brown, "Memories."
50. Ibid.
51. Radke-Moss, *Bright Epoch*.
52. Brown, "Memories"
53. Ibid.
54. Ibid.
55. Ibid.
56. Barry, *Great Influenza*.
57. "Red Cross Nutrition Course," *Box Elder News*.
58. "Business Women Score Ban on Working Wives," *Salt Lake Telegram*.

Chapter 17

59. Pinborough, "Minerva Kohlhepp Teichert."
60. Gardner, "Painting the Mormon Story."
61. Ibid.

Chapter 18

62. Arias and Free, "Tireless Kuniko Terasawa."

Chapter 19

63. "Marjorie Redding Christiansen, 44-W-3."
64. Reichman, "Utah WWII Flygirl."

Chapter 20

65. "A Life Full of Service," *Deseret News*.

Chapter 21

66. The Cleveland Cultural Gardens Federation.
67. "Ruey Hazlet Wiesley."
68. Clark, "Alice Kasai."
69. International Peace Gardens National Register of Historic Places Registration Form.

Chapter 22

70. Mazuran, "'Story Princess' Visits."
71. Whitney, "After 54 Years, Illustrated Songbook."
72. "Story Princess Introduces Her Radio Show."

Chapter 23

73. Jan Shipps, foreword, in Brooks, *Mountain Meadows Massacre*.
74. Brooks, *Mountain Meadows Massacre*.

Chapter 24

75. Priest, *Green Grows Ivy*.
76. Ibid., 295.
77. "Be Not Fooled Utah Voters," *Davis County Clipper*.

Chapter 25

78. Bankhead, Oral History.
79. Ibid.
80. Ibid.

Chapter 26

81. Ferguson, "If I Were 21."
82. Papanikolas, "Growing Up Greek," 257–59.

Chapter 27

83. Okazaki, *Lighten Up!*, 7.
84. Prince, "'There Is Always a Struggle,'" 112–40.
85. Stack, "Beloved Mormon Women's Leader Chieko Okazaki Dies."

Chapter 28

86. Ingram, "Inspiring True Story Behind the LDS Hymn."
87. Pendley, "Woman of Gentle Strength."
88. Thayne, *Place of Knowing*.

Chapter 29

89. Toomer, "We Were Pretty Edgy," 385.
90. Toomer, Oral History.
91. Toomer, "We Were Pretty Edgy," 386.
92. Toomer, Oral History.

BIBLIOGRAPHY

Anagnostou, Yiorgos. "Helen Zeese Papanikolas." Preservation of American Hellenic History. www.pahh.com/news/news027.html.

Arias, Ron, and Cathy Free, "Tireless Kuniko Terasawa Is the Force Behind a Newspaper Almost No One Can Read." *People*, September 25, 1989.

Ashby, David A. "Kate B. Carter." Icelandic National League of North America. April 10, 2014. www.inlofna.org/font-style=font-size-12px-face=Tahoma.

Aton, James M. *John Wesley Powell.* Boise State University Western Writers Series no. 114. Boise, ID: Boise State University Press, 1994.

Babcock, Maud May. "Pantomime." *Proceedings of the National Association of Elocutionists.* Cincinnati, OH: Douglas A. Brown, 1898, 223–24.

"Bankhead, Mary Lucille Perkins (1902–1994)." African American History in the West. BlackPast.org.

Bankhead, Mary Lucille Perkins. Oral History, interview by Alan Cherry, typescript, LDS Afro-American Oral History Project by the Charles Redd Center for Western Studies, April 11, 1985.

Barkhorn, Eleanor. "'Vote No on Women's Suffrage': Bizarre Reasons for Not Letting Women Vote." *The Atlantic*, November 6, 2012.

Barry, John M. *The Great Influenza.* New York: Penguin Books, 2005.

Box Elder News. "Red Cross Nutrition Course." April 17, 1925.

"Bridget 'Biddy' Mason." National Park Service. www.nps.gov/people/biddymason.htm.

Brooks, Juanita. *The Mountain Meadows Massacre*. Norman: University of Oklahoma Press, 1991.

Brown, Almeda Perry. "Memories." Typescript, Leonard J. Arrington Papers, 1839–1999. Utah State University, Merrill-Cazier Library, Special Collections and Archives Division.

Brulliard, Nicholas. "Wild West Josie." National Parks Conservation Association. Winter 2017. www.npca.org/articles/1417-wild-west-josie.

Bunch, Joey. "Colorado's Wild Women Left Their Not-So-Delicate Brand on Wild West's Outlaw Lore." Denver Post: The Archive, September 30, 2012. blogs.denverpost.com/library/2012/09/30/colorados-wild-women-left-notsodelicate-brand-wild-wests-outlaw-lore/3960.

Carter, D. Robert. "Josie Bassett—Jensen's Remarkable Woman Rancher." *History Blazer*, December 1996. historytogo.utah.gov/utah_chapters/pioneers_and_cowboys/josiebassett.html.

Clark, Cody. "Aviation Pioneer, Film Subject Made Little-Remembered Utah Visit." *Daily Herald*, October 21, 2009.

Clark, Rebekah. "Alice Kasai, Believer in the Oneness of Humankind." Better Days 2020. www.utahwomenshistory.org/bios/alice-kasai.

The Cleveland Cultural Gardens Federation. www.clevelandculturalgardens.org/gardens/american-legion.

Coleman, Ronald G. "Blacks in Utah: An Unknown Legacy." *Peoples of Utah*. historytogo.utah.gov/people/ethnic_cultures/the_peoples_of_utah/blacksinutahhistory.html.

Collins, Lois M. "Alive Again—Emma Lou Thayne Finds Hope, Recovery and a Vibrant Life." *Deseret News*, January 15, 2011.

Cooper-Rompato, Christine. "Women Inventors in Utah Territory." *Utah Historical Quarterly* 83, no. 3 (Summer 2015).

Davis County Clipper. "Be Not Fooled Utah Voters, Says Ivy Baker Priest." November 3, 1950.

Derr, Jill Mulvay, et al. *The First Fifty Years of Relief Society*. Salt Lake City, UT: Church Historian's Press, 2016.

Deseret News. "A Life Full of Service." June 14, 1973.

Dobner, Jennifer. "She Was a Teen Mother, a High School Dropout and an Onion Field Worker—Now She's Utah's First Female Sheriff." *Salt Lake Tribune*, December 17, 2017.

Eureka Reporter. "Miss Maude Fitch of Eureka Is Awarded French Cross." July 19, 1918.

Ferguson, Melba B. "If I Were 21." *Salt Lake Tribune*, September 5, 1948.

Fields, Lauren. "How a Mormon Pioneer Woman Became the Nation's First Female State Senator." *Deseret News*, November 2, 2017.

Gardner, Peter B. "Painting the Mormon Story." *BYU Magazine*, Winter 2008.

Gehrke, Robert. "Barbara Toomer Was a Relentless Advocate for Fair Treatment for Utah's Disabled and a Role Model for the Rest of Us." *Salt Lake Tribune*, April 25, 2018.

Graña, Mari. *Pioneer, Polygamist, Politician: The Life of Dr. Martha Hughes Cannon.* TwoDot, 2009.

Hafen, P. Jane. "A Cultural Duet: Zitkála-Šá and *The Sun Dance Opera*." *Great Plains Quarterly* (Spring 1998): 102–11.

Hall, Andrew. "In Memorium—Emma Lou Thayne." *Dawning of a Brighter Day*, December 7, 2014.

Hall, Sharon. "Feisty Female Sheriffs: Claire Helena Ferguson, in Her Own Words." *Digging History*, October 16, 2015.

Hanson, Kathleen S. "Down to Vicksburg: The Nurses' Experience." *Journal of the Illinois State Historical Society* 97, no. 4 (Winter 2004–5): 286–309.

Haynes, Mark. "Historic Utah Female Government to Be Honored on Centennial." *Salt Lake Tribune*, January 26, 2012.

Helm, Elsie. "Reminiscence," Typescript. www.ancestry.com/mediaui-viewer/tree/24976096/person/1878084477/media/71da894d-087c-45e0-8143-95465bc08fc9?_phsrc=m3v-1457998&_phstart=successSource.

Hull, LeAnne von Neumeyer. "Bridget 'Biddy' Smith Mason: Her Legacy Among the Mormons." Black Voice News. blackvoicenews.com/2006/03/24/bridget-biddy-smith-mason-her-legacy-among-the-mormons.

Iber, Jorge. *Hispanics in the Mormon Zion, 1912–1999.* College Station: Texas A&M University Press, 2000.

Iber, Jorge, and Arnoldo DeLeon. *Hispanics in the American West.* Santa Barbara, CA: ABC-CLIO, 2006.

Ingram, Aleah. "The Inspiring True Story Behind the LDS Hymn, 'Where Can I Turn for Peace?'" *LDS Daily*, October 4, 2016. www.ldsdaily.com/personal-lds-blog/inspiring-true-story-behind-lds-hymn-can-turn-peace.

International Peace Gardens National Register of Historic Places Registration Form. www.slcdocs.com/Planning/HLC/2014/peace.pdf.

Intravartolo, Cindy. "St. Mary's Goes to War: The Sisters of the Holy Cross as Civil War Nurses." *Journal of the Illinois State Historical Society* 107, nos. 3–4 (Fall/Winter 2014): 370–91.

Iverson, Wayne. "Chipeta: A Detailed History." Chipeta Mountain Project. February 27, 2016. www.chipetamountain.com/journal/2016/2/27/a-more-detailed-history.

Jones, J.A. "The Sun Dance of the Northern Ute." Smithsonian Institution Bureau of American Ethnology Bulletin 157.

"Kuniko Muramatsu Terasawa." Utah History to Go. historytogo.utah.gov/people/utahns_of_achievement/kunikomuramatsuterasawa.html.

Lieber, Constance L., and John Sillito. *Letters from Exile: The Correspondence of Martha Hughes Cannon and Angus M. Cannon, 1886–1888*. Salt Lake City, UT: Signature Books, 1989.

Lyman-Whitney, Susan. "Chipeta." *Deseret News*, October 16, 1994.

———. "Greek Migration to Utah." *Deseret News*, September 3, 1993.

Lythgoe, Dennis Leo. "Negro Slavery in Utah." Master's thesis, University of Utah, 1966.

"Marjorie Redding Christiansen, 44-W-3." WASP Final Flight. waspfinalflight.blogspot.com/2009/02/wasp-marjorie-redding-christiansen-44-w.html.

"Martha Hughes Cannon." KUED Productions. www.kued.org/whatson/kued-productions/martha-hughes-cannon.

Mason, Carol Cornwall. "Emmeline B. Wells: A Fine Soul Who Served." *Ensign*, July 2003.

Mazuran, Evelyn. "'Story Princess' Visits." *Deseret News*. Undated article in family's possession likely from the late 1960s.

Mooney, Bernice M., and Miriam M. Murphy. "Sister Augusta and Catholic Education in Utah." *History Blazer*, June 1996. historytogo.utah.gov/utah_chapters/mining_and_railroads/sisteraugustaandcatholiceducationinutah.html.

Murphy, Miriam B. "World War I Heroine Maud Fitch Lived in Eureka, Utah." *History Blazer*, April 1995. historytogo.utah.gov/utah_chapters/from_war_to_war/worldwar1heroinemaudfitchlivedineurekautah.html.

Niiya, Brian. "Utah Nippo (newspaper)." Densho Encyclopedia. January 12, 2018. encyclopedia.densho.org/Utah_Nippo_(newspaper).

Northrup, Henry Davenport. *The World's Fair as Seen in One Hundred Days*. Philadelphia: National Publishing Company, 1893.

Okazaki, Chieko. *Lighten Up!* Salt Lake City, UT: Deseret Book, 1993.

"Orlando Rivera, University of Utah Diversity Pioneer, Dies." Campus Life from the U, February 16, 2006. archive.unews.utah.edu/news_releases/orlando-rivera-university-of-utah-diversity-pioneer-dies.

Papanikolas, Helen Z. "The Exiled Greeks." *Peoples of Utah*. historytogo.utah.gov/people/ethnic_cultures/the_peoples_of_utah/theexiledgreeks.html.

———. "Growing Up Greek in Helper, Utah." *Utah Historical Quarterly* 48 (Summer 1980): 257–59.

———. "Magerou: The Greek Midwife." *Utah Historical Quarterly* 38, no. 1 (1970): 50–60.

Pendley, Nettie. "A Woman of Gentle Strength." *Continuum* 12, no. 3 (Winter 2002–2003).

Pinborough, Jan Underwood. "Minerva Kohlhepp Teichert: With a Bold Brush," *Ensign*, April 1989.

Priest, Ivy Baker. *Green Grows Ivy.* New York: McGraw-Hill, 1958.

Prince, Gregory N. "'There Is Always a Struggle': An Interview with Chieko N. Okazaki." *Dialogue: A Journal of Mormon Thought* 45, no. 1 (Spring 2012): 112–40.

Radke-Moss, Andrea G. *Bright Epoch: Women and Coeducation in the American West.* Lincoln: University of Nebraska Press, 2008.

Ratliffe, Sharon A. "Maud May Babcock (1867–1954): President during the National Communication Association's 21st Year, 1936." *Review of Communication* 5, no. 1 (2005): 56–62.

Reeder, Jennifer Reeder, and Kate Holbrook. "Thirteenth Ward Relief Society Covenant." *At the Pulpit.* Salt Lake City: The Church Historian's Press, 2017.

Reeve, W. Paul. "Ivy Baker Priest: A Bingham High Coed Rose to the Post of U.S. Treasurer." *History Blazer*, June 1995. historytogo.utah.gov/people/ivybakerpriest.html.

———. "Just Who Was the Outlaw Queen Etta Place?" *History Blazer*, May 1995. historytogo.utah.gov/utah_chapters/pioneers_and_cowboys/justwhowastheoutlawqueenettaplace.html.

Reichman, Matt. "Utah WWII Flygirl Finally Gets Her Due." *Daily Herald*, April 2, 2010.

Rivera de Martinez, Domitila. Oral History. Interview by Gordon Irving, 1975, typescript, James Moyle Oral History Program, Archives, Historical Department of the Church of Jesus Christ of Latter-day Saints, Salt Lake City, Utah. Translated by Daniel Wheeler.

"Ruey Hazlet Wiesley." Utah History to Go. historytogo.utah.gov/people/utahns_of_achievement/rueyhazletwiesley.html.

Salt Lake Telegram. "Business Women Score Ban on Working Wives." May 20, 1939.

———. "Miss Alene Olsen's Betrothal to Ross F. Dalton Revealed." October 29, 1938.

Salt Lake Tribune. "Miss Claire Ferguson." June 23, 1897.

———. "Miss Maud Fitch, Utah Heroine, Is Home, Wears War Cross and Stars for Bravery." May 2, 1919.

———. "The Nurse Goes Free." December 7, 1898.

———. "She Has Power to Arrest." July 14, 1899.

———. "Some Startling Charges." August 9, 1894, 8.

———. "Stricken Aviators Rushed to Hospital." October 7, 1918.

———. "Wounded Americans Superb Maintain Spirit When Hurt." October 6, 1918.

Skinner, Cecilia. "Honoring a Heritage: Exhibit Celebrates First Mexican Latter-day Saints in Utah." *Deseret News*, November 20, 2012.

Smith, Joseph F. "Maud May Babcock 1867–1954." *The Speech Teacher* 11, no. 2 (1962): 105–7.

Snodgrass, Mary Ellen. *Frontier Women and Their Art*. London: Rowman and Littlefield, 2018.

Stack, Peggy Fletcher. "Beloved Mormon Women's Leader Chieko Okazaki Dies," *Salt Lake Tribune*, August 5, 2011.

Stamberg, Susan. "Female WWII Pilots: The Original Fly Girls." NPR Morning Edition. March 9, 2010. www.npr.org/2010/03/09/123773525/female-wwii-pilots-the-original-fly-girls.

"The Story Princess Introduces Her Radio Show." University of Utah, J. Willard Marriott Library Multimedia Archives. www.youtube.com/watch?v=72l7-Ld_BPk.

Tanner, John S. "Shakespeare Among the Saints." *Journal of Mormon History* 21, no. 1 (Spring 2006): 82–115.

Thayne, Emma Lou. *The Place of Knowing*. Bloomington, IN: iUniverse, 2011.

Thompson, Dr. Jackie. "Mignon Barker Richmond, A Community Organizer with Heart." Better Days 2020. www.utahwomenshistory.org/bios/mignon-barker-richmond.

Toomer, Barbara Greenlee. Oral History. Interview by Becky B. Lloyd. Everett L. Cooley Oral History Project, University of Utah J. Willard Marriott Library.

———. "We Were Pretty Edgy, for Salt Lake City." In *What We Have Done: An Oral History of the Disability Rights Movement*, edited by Fred Pelka. Amherst: University of Massachusetts Press, 2012.

Topping, Gary. "A Utah Catholic Woman in World War I." *Intermountain Catholic*, June 15, 2018. www.icatholic.org/article/a-tribute-to-mother-augusta-csc-79511414.

Trimble, Marshall. "Tangled Webs: The Wild Bunch and Their Women." *True West*, January 30, 2017.

Turley, Kylie Nielson. "Kanab's All Woman Town Council, 1912–1914: Politics, Power Struggles, and Polygamy." *Utah Historical Quarterly* 73, no. 4 (Fall 2005): 308–28.

Van Leer, Twila. "Industrious Sister Augusta Was Surprise to Utahns." *Deseret News*, July 9, 1996.

Wells, Emmeline B. Diaries, 1844–1920: electronic resource, vol. 1. Special Collections, Harold B. Lee Library, Brigham Young University Library, Provo. contentdm.lib.byu.edu/digital/collection/Diaries/id/4267.

Whitney, Susan. "After 54 Years, Illustrated Songbook Keeps Holding Children's Attention." *Deseret News*, April 26, 2001.

Williams, Carter. "Remembering Utah's Forgotten Black Pioneers." KSL.com, February 22, 2018. www.ksl.com/article/46267076.

Worster, David. *A River Running West*. Oxford: Oxford University Press, 2001.

"Zitkála-Šá." Early Native American Literature. nativeamericanwriters.com/zitkala-sa.html.

"Zitkála-Šá Red Bird." Akta Lakota Museum & Cultural Center. aktalakota.stjo.org/site/News2?page=NewsArticle&id=8882.

INDEX

A

African Americans 26, 117, 120,
    145, 152
Anthony, Susan B. 19, 23

B

Babcock, Maud May 73–78, 101
Bankhead, Mary Lucille Perkins
    145–149
Bassett, Ann 55–59
Bassett, Josie 55–59
Bonnin, Gertrude Simmons.
    See Zitkála-Šá
Bosone, Reva Beck 142
Brigham City, Utah 83, 128, 131
Brigham Young University 77, 109,
    136, 151
Brooks, Juanita Leavitt 135–139
Brown, Almeda Perry 99–105
Brunot, Felix R. 15

Busby, Matilda Dudley 31–36
Bushnell General Military Hospital
    128
Butch Cassidy's Wild Bunch 56,
    62, 99

C

Cannon, Martha Hughes 49–54,
    60, 84
Carson, Kit 15
Carter, Kate Bearnson 150–152
Castle Gate, Utah 152
Catholics in Utah 38, 89, 96
Cedar City, Utah 102, 138
Chamberlain, Mary Woolley 84
Chicago World's Fair 24, 48
Chipeta 13–18
Christiansen, Marjorie Redding
    116–119
Church of Jesus Christ of Latter-day
    Saints 11, 13, 21, 24, 27, 29,

32, 34, 37, 50, 52, 77, 94, 97,
98, 101, 109, 119, 139, 147,
152, 156, 158, 159, 161, 162
Civil War 27, 38, 44

D

Dalton, Alene 131–134
Daughters of Utah Pioneers 145, 151
Devoto, Bernard 39
Dixie State University 136
Downwinders 163

E

Earhart, Amelia 88

F

Ferguson, Claire 60–63
Fitch, Maud 88–93

G

Gates, Susa Young 19, 73
Genesis Group 148
Grant, Ulysses S. 16, 38, 45
Great Depression 59, 106, 136,
142, 165

H

Hamblin, Blanche Robinson 85
Hamblin, Tamar Stewart 85

healthcare 23, 35, 39, 41, 44, 48,
50, 53, 60, 66, 89, 103, 108,
149, 154, 165, 166
Helper, Utah 152
Howard, Mary. *See* Chamberlain,
Mary Woolley

I

influenza pandemic 96, 103, 109

J

James, Jane Manning 27, 145
Japanese American Citizens League
113, 130, 155

K

Kanab, Utah 48, 84
Kasai, Alice 128
Kimberly, Utah 140
Ku Klux Klan 69, 152

L

Logan, Utah 101, 103
Lynn, Utah 99

M

Magerou, Georgia Lathouris 64–69
Mason, Biddy 26–30
McAllister, Luella Atkin 85

mental illness 62, 103, 104, 160, 161

mining 13, 15, 36, 37, 64, 88, 140, 152, 163

Monticello, Utah 96

Mother Mary Augusta 37–41

Mountain Meadows Massacre 34, 135

N

NAACP 122, 123, 168

Native Americans 13, 31, 33, 37, 45, 47, 71, 79, 82, 83, 109, 135, 138, 163

O

Ogden, Utah 107

Okazaki, Chieko Nishimura 156–160

Ouray 14

P

Papanikolas, Helen Zeese 152–155

Parowan, Utah 119

Place, Etta 56

polygamy 22, 34, 50, 94, 101, 125, 139

Powell, Emma Dean 42–48

Powell, John Wesley 42

Priest, Ivy Baker 140–144

Prohibition 59, 85

Provo, Utah 100, 110, 136

R

Red Cross 89, 103, 122, 128, 144

Relief Society 25, 33, 97, 148, 158, 167

Richmond, Mignon Barker 120–123

Rivera de Martinez, Domitila 94–98

S

Salt Lake City 22, 28, 33, 35, 36, 37, 47, 50, 60, 77, 86, 94, 102, 106, 114, 120, 122, 127, 131, 145, 151, 152, 154, 156, 162, 167

Seegmiller, Ada Pratt 85

Shipp, Ellis R. 50, 60

Smith, Joseph 21, 26, 34, 135, 145

Snow, Eliza R. 34, 50, 152

Stegner, Wallace 71

St. George, Utah 136

T

Teichert, Minerva 106–110

Terasawa, Kuniko Muramatsu 112–115

Thayne, Emma Lou 161–164

Toomer, Barbara Greenlee 165–169

U

Ulrich, Laurel Thatcher 139, 162

University of Utah 73, 98, 114, 122, 131, 142, 151, 154, 156, 161, 169

Utah State University 104, 120, 123
Utah War 34, 135, 139

V

Vernal, Utah 59, 81, 99

W

Wells, Emmeline B. 19–25, 50, 52,
    60
Wiesley, Ruey Hazlet 127–130
Williams, Terry Tempest 163
Woman's Exponent 23, 50, 60
women's suffrage 74, 82, 84, 88,
    108
World War I 25, 82, 88, 102, 108,
    127
World War II 82, 98, 105, 111, 116,
    122, 127, 131, 154, 156, 162

Y

Young, Brigham 22, 27, 33, 37, 39,
    47, 50, 73, 136
Young Men's Christian Association
    89, 122
Young Women's General Board
    158, 161

Z

Zitkála-Šá 79–83

ABOUT THE AUTHOR

Emily Brooksby Wheeler attended Brigham Young University, majoring in history with an English minor, and earned graduate degrees in history and landscape architecture from Utah State University. She's the award-winning author of several historical novels, including *Born to Treason*, *No Peace with the Dawn* (with Jeffery Bateman) and *Letters from the Homefront*, as well as short stories, magazine articles and scripts for educational software programs. She's an adjunct professor of Utah history at USU and a museum collections specialist for the Bushnell, Intermountain and USU exhibit. She lives in northern Utah with her family.

Visit us at
www.historypress.com
....